SCAM!

HOW TO AVOID THE SCAMS THAT COST VICTIMS BILLIONS OF DOLLARS EVERY YEAR

By

HOPE OJE

www.scam-thebook.com

Table of Contents

PROLOGUE

The YouTube algorithm is an incredible thing.

In the midst of the global Coronavirus pandemic, YouTube took me down a very interesting rabbit hole. Of all the things I discovered in Spring 2020, **scambaiting** was the most captivating.

Every industry has an ecosystem, and the scam industry is no different. Within this industry, you have the scammers who deceive people into giving them hundreds, thousands, or even millions of dollars. And you have the victims who, lacking important information, surrender their money for little to no real benefit.

This ecosystem generates billions of dollars every year, making it lucrative for scammers and worth the risk of legal action, as scammers are often able to get away with breaking the law in this way (CNBC 2021).

A growing portion of this ecosystem is the scambaiter population.

Scambaiters have one goal in mind: to waste as much of a scammer's time as possible. I will provide examples of the scambaiters I discovered via the YouTube algorithm later in this book but for now, understand that scambaiters are people who disrupt scam operations to reduce the amount of time in a day scammers have to reach real, potential victims.

The slower a scammer can work, the less money they are able to make from innocent people who would fall for their scam. There is no guarantee of this, but this is still the goal.

Scamming is a numbers game.

Scammers know not everyone is gullible. However, if they move quickly, they're able to weed out the people who won't fall for their scams so they can move on to more vulnerable people who are willing to empty their pockets into the scammer's fraudulent accounts.

The more I watched how these scam operations worked, and the more I learned about how big this industry is, how much money innocent people were losing, and how devastating those losses were for not only the victims but also their family members, the more I felt called to do something.

I started picking up every phone call I had time for. While I usually recommend not answering the phone to potential scammers, and I'll talk about why in a subsequent chapter, I wanted to be a part of the solution.

I dove headfirst into scambaiting with the goal of wasting as much of the scammer's time as possible, which, for me, came out to around 20-30 minutes per call—a far cry from the 36+ hours YouTube scambaiters like Kitboga (mentioned in more detail later) are able to accomplish. My 20 minutes pale in comparison to his 36+ hours.

But scammers proclaim they can move through victims in five to ten minutes or less, so I was at least happy to keep them tied up for the time it would normally take them to steal money from three to six victims.

Unfortunately, there's only so much I can do by tying up one scammer at a time for only 30 minutes a day. With hundreds, if not thousands, of scammers out there pursuing people daily, my 30-minute distraction is laughable at best.

That's why I decided to write this book. I discovered the scambaiting community online, completely by accident, as I was watching music videos, documentaries, and other random clips.

By chance, a random title piqued my interest, and that's how I came to know about different scambaiters. While I'm glad I know they exist, I also understand that some people may never find that corner of the internet where scambaiters entertain, vindicate victims, and wreak havoc on scammers and their call centers.

I'm sure there are a lot of people who don't watch YouTube videos. Many people even today don't have a stable or reliable internet connection. And of those who do, how many will ever stumble upon a Jim Browning video?

Many, but not nearly enough.

And of those who do stumble onto these videos, how many would be susceptible to the scams explored in the videos?

Not many.

Many of the viewers are already skeptical of scams and aren't the scammer's target.

For those who watch YouTube, there's some chance they'll randomly find a scambait video. But for those who don't watch YouTube or Twitch or other platforms where scambaiters share their content, how will they know what's going on?

My goal, aside from spreading more awareness, is to reach the people who might not stumble upon a video, but who may stumble upon this book.

There's a misconception that scammers only target "old people," but that couldn't be farther from the truth. A scammer is willing and able to scam anyone who's vulnerable enough to listen, and desperate enough for a solution to trust the scammer's proposition.

Falling for a scam has everything to do with vulnerability and a lack of knowledge, and nothing to do with age or demographic background, though some populations may be more susceptible to being victimized than others, depending on the scam.

With an understanding that spreading awareness is the best way to prevent more people from losing money they might not be able to afford, over the course of this book, I will discuss 30+ types of scams circulating right now.

While there are many more scams and scam spinoffs out there, I believe these 30+ scams are the most frequently encountered and knowing the ins and outs of these ones will help people spot red flags to look out for when sussing out other potential scams.

Chapter 1. Introduction

Did you know scamming is a billion-dollar industry?

In 2021, scammers made out with an estimated $30 billion dollars from phone call scams directed at residents of the United States of America, alone. Knowing this $30 billion statistic only accounts for one scam medium and not email, text, or social media, and considers information from only one country, makes it that much more alarming.

Though scammers target several different countries all over the world, their scams tend to be the most successful in America, Canada, the United Kingdom, and Australia. This could be because these are predominantly English-speaking countries, and most scammers are able to speak in conversational English at the very least.

Scam scripts do exist in other languages like Spanish, German, and French, for example. But when a scammer isn't well-versed in the language their script is written in, potential scam victims who do speak that language tend to be wary. And even if the potential victim is not suspicious of a stranger calling and struggling through their language, if they have difficulty understanding the scammer, they are likely to just hang up the phone.

It's not just Americans who suffer. In the UK, romance scammers made off with over £73.9 million from victims during the recent coronavirus pandemic (Which? 2021).

Who knows how much more revenue scam calls generate when we combine the figures from all countries being targeted?

If you have been targeted by a scam and you live in America, the UK, or another predominantly English-speaking country, you're not alone. Millions of people are targeted by these scams every year. And that number continues to increase year after year because not enough people are educated about the diverse types of scams and the way they work to be able to recognize a scam when they encounter them.

There are many people who call scammers and engage with them to waste their time so potential victims are saved, at least temporarily. And some people even get paid to do this. But that, alone, is not enough to stop this growing problem.

That's where this book, and hopefully many more resources like it, comes in.

Over the course of this book, one of my goals is to teach you what different types of scams exist so you know what to look out for and how to avoid falling for those scams, yourself.

The second goal of this book is to show you that anyone can fall for a scam. Stereotypically, it's believed that only older people (above 60 years of age) fall for these scams because they're not mentally agile enough to know better. Anyone in their right mind can recognize when something sounds fraudulent, right?

Well, it's not that simple.

The only truth in this line of reasoning has nothing to do with age. The truth in this train of thought is if a scammer can catch you in a moment where you lose touch with your logical reasoning skills, they can trick you into doing almost anything. Thus, you have strayed from your "right mind" due to a vulnerability or pain point a scammer is able to exploit and use to their advantage.

But age, itself, does not matter.

All it takes for someone to fall for a scam is for the scam to be relevant and timely. That's why many immigrants are targeted with immigration-related scams, which I'll discuss in more detail in the next chapter.

Anyone can fall for a scam, but you're much less likely to fall for one if you know what the red flags and warning signs look like. In this book, I will describe over 30+ common scams in detail, describing how they work and what each scam's intention is.

Additionally, in the Appendix, I will provide samples of scam call scripts, scam text messages I have received, scam email samples, and scam voicemail scripts to further illustrate what these scams look like in the real world.

Armed with this knowledge, you'll be better equipped to prevent yourself from falling victim to a scam and contributing to the growing annual revenue for scam operations around the world.

Over the course of a year, people will lose billions of dollars in life savings, retirement money, social security checks, and other funds they depend on to live to people who get up every day to work at companies that prosper by stealing and providing no benefits to consumers, only pain and devastation.

Unfortunately, people will continue to be taken advantage of and lose their money in this way until they know what to watch out for.

CHAPTER 2. COMMON TYPES OF SCAMS

PRINCE SCAM

These were a lot more popular at the onset of the Internet, back in the late 90s to early 2000s. This scam seemed to circulate most to Yahoo email addresses. But since it's a popular scam and, potentially, one of the oldest scams in circulation, I think it's worth mentioning. If you haven't received one of these emails in a very long time, that doesn't mean it's not still going around.

On the contrary, this scam has evolved in some subtle ways.

The premise of this scam is that a member of an international royal family or high-ranking government official has access to a large sum of money. In past iterations of this scam, the prince wanted to just give you millions of dollars with no strings attached. But now, the scam has changed.

Instead, the prince or high-ranking official needs to move some money out of the country and/or out of his bank account. But because his account is being monitored (or is facing money transfer limitations), the prince is counting on you to assist.

If you agree to help, the prince will transfer millions of dollars into your account, with the goal of transferring that money elsewhere once he has safely moved it out of his account. In exchange for allowing the prince to use your bank account to move the money, he will give you a portion of the funds, as a thank-you.

Sounds like an easy way to make a whole lot of cash. But of course, it's an easy way to lose your bank account and all the money in it instead.

With access to your account, scammers will transfer all your money into their account(s). If they're sufficiently able to lock you out of your account, they'll also use it for money laundering. Scammers are often smart enough to not use their own personal bank accounts. Instead, they create foreign accounts to use for stealing money, or they'll use stolen accounts to do all the dirty work.

Yes, princes, princesses, queens, and other distinguished officials do exist. But the chance might as well be zero that one of these individuals will reach out to you, someone who they do not know, to assist them with what sounds like money laundering (Leonhardt, 2019).

Romance Scam

Aside from survival, one of the biggest motivating forces a human being has is love.

Humans are prone to feeling lonely, even when we don't want to admit it. Even when we do have access to love, for many people, it can feel insufficient, or even like it isn't there at all.

Romance scammers don't know who exactly is experiencing loneliness, but they know if they message enough people on social media, eventually they'll find some good candidates.

Though this scam knows no age limit, many romance scammers concentrate a lot of their time on older men and women, especially those who post pictures without any trace of a significant other.

When you've spent a lifetime with someone and they pass away, it's devastating. It can be so hard to find the right romantic fit. And to have that connection vanish is nothing short of traumatic.

Romance scammers hope to fill that void, or at least trick you into believing they can. Romance scammers thrive on social media, so be wary when you get random friend and follow requests.

In an age where social media is the thing that connects us all, it's not uncommon for random people to find us on social media and want to connect. So, romance scammers send out friend requests across Facebook, Instagram, Twitter, and all sorts of other sites, using fake pictures they hope will be appealing to their potential victims. From there, a romance scammer will try to strike up a conversation with you to gauge how open and receptive you'll be to their advances.

Unfortunately, you have no idea who the person on the other end of that profile is. You know nothing about who they are, where they're from, what they actually look like, etc. Though the compliments can sound nice and authentic, that scammer isn't actually forging a real romantic relationship with you.

The romance scammer's goal is to make you comfortable with them. Once you're comfortable, the scammer starts asking you for money, or at least hinting that they need some. Once you've fallen in love with the person you thought you were talking to, they hope you just might cash out your retirement income for them.

Do you really care about your loved one's well-being if you aren't there in a desperate time of need? The scammer wants to know how loyal you will be.

When he finds out he has cancer and needs $10,000 for chemotherapy, will you send the money via Western Union?

When her mom's diabetes medication runs out and she needs $2,000 to get more, will you send the money via PayPal?

When his car breaks down and prevents him from going to work, will you Cash App him $300 to fix it?

It doesn't matter if you have extra money to spare, or not. If you don't send the money, or if you were sending money but you decide to stop, you'll lose your sweetheart for sure.

Romance scammers invest a lot of time into making you feel secure in the relationship, so they tend to stick around and be persistent. But after several failed requests for money, the scammer will move on to someone else who might be more likely to send the money they are after.

If you do send money to a romance scammer and then discover the truth, who will you tell? The embarrassment ensures you won't tell a single soul. That helps romance scammers get away with this. No one wants to feel judged for being taken advantage of, especially not romantically and monetarily (FBI, 2020).

PHILANTHROPY SCAM

You receive an email from Bill Gates, Mark Zuckerberg, or some other incredibly accomplished billionaire.

This communication is out-of-the-blue. You've never actually met this wealthy person before. But you've heard of him.

You read the email from Mr. Bill Gates, and in that email, he explains that he'd like to give you several million dollars to distribute to charitable causes you deem worthy of a generous donation from Mr. Bill Gates, himself.

Of course, this is a scam.

I don't know what the success rate is of any of the scams that are detailed in this book, but I venture to guess this particular scam has a very low success rate, if for no other reason than the email address sending the communication does not match the high-profile individual's name, or that of any organization the billionaire is associated with.

The chances seem slim that Mark Zuckerberg would email strangers from a Gmail account that isn't even associated with his name.

But aside from the email address not matching the name of the person, it's also hard to believe that a wealthy, high-profile individual who has access to financial advisors and who most likely has causes they care about already would reach out to a complete stranger offering large sums of money to do whatever they want with.

Yet the email aims to make you feel special; you are the chosen one. After much deliberation, you came out on top, or so the email may lead you to believe. Now, to claim all that money, you just have to submit your bank account information to Bill Gates and he'll wire the funds directly into your account.

In some instances, Bill Gates may require you to pay a fee in order to access this multi-million-dollar fund.

But what's a few hundred dollars if it means you have access to millions?

But here's the problem with that fee: If Mark Zuckerberg can afford to give you, someone who he's never met before, $10 million to do with as you please, why wouldn't he be able to cover the $200-$500 fee required to dispatch those millions of dollars?

If you can refrain from acting hastily, you'll find several more holes in this storyline that indicate it's too good to be true.

BLACKMAIL SCAM

One random morning, I received an email telling me that if I didn't send Bitcoin to the Bitcoin wallet specified in the email, the self-identified hacker would share footage of me watching porn with all my friends, family, and co-workers.

The person claimed he had video evidence of me that he obtained by hacking into my laptop camera and splitting the screen so he could see the pornography I was watching, as well as me and my physical responses to the pornography. With this footage, he planned to embarrass me and ruin my reputation if I didn't send thousands of dollars' worth of Bitcoin.

There were several problems with this threat. The biggest one?

I don't watch porn.

This scammer also failed to mention any name or personal information that would indicate he even knew who I was. And the email was written so vaguely, it was obviously a mass email sent to who knows how many people.

These blackmail scams don't always have to be about porn, but they do tend to be about taboo topics. This type of scam may have worked if it landed in the inbox of someone who does watch porn and was worried about other people finding out.

If you're involved in any kind of taboo activity and you're worried about what that could do to your reputation if people found out, this scammer may have had you right where they wanted you.

Two things make this scam potentially more effective than most. First of all, the email had a password I've used before as the subject line of the email. While the body of the email was very generic, seeing my password in the title did make me think I was being targeted by someone who knew me, at least for a second.

But it's important to understand that data breaches happen frequently, so that password was probably very easy to find. And if your password is the only piece of information the person has about you, especially if it was a password that was exposed in a data breach, the chances are high that the person who sent you the email doesn't actually know who you are.

The second thing that makes this scam potentially more effective than most is the threat to share a dark secret you hold to people whose opinions matter to you. For many, depending on what the secret is, this can be incredibly scary and anxiety-inducing.

Free Car Scam

You get a text message that says you won a free Lamborghini. All you have to do is confirm all your personal details and submit a picture of your identification. You don't even have to pay a fee to claim your prize.

Score!

But once you submit everything that's requested of you, your information is sold to other scammers. Sending a photo of your ID also leaves you vulnerable to identity theft.

Also, maybe this goes without saying, but there is no free car after you hand over your identity for free.

You may not consider giving someone your name, phone number, and even your address to be much of a big deal. In fact, that information is already available publicly.

But these scammers will also ask for a picture of your identification. And with that, they have everything they need to apply for or falsify passports and other forms of identification in your name. Once they do that, aside from selling your information to other scammers for profit, they can also commit all sorts of crimes under your name that you may have little to no control over once your information gets into the wrong person's hands.

If the scammer is based in your home country, it may be easier to stop them in their tracks. But even with identity protection software and services, if pictures of your identification get into the hands of an international scammer who's not under the same jurisdiction as you, it can be incredibly difficult to stop them.

Should it happen to you, you can and should report identity theft to the major credit card bureaus, your financial institutions, and local authorities. But you will have a hard time tracking down and reporting the actual person who compromised your information because you don't know who they are.

All you have is a fake name and a phone number that may not be linked to them in any way, as phone numbers are very easy to acquire and dump when no longer needed.

If you're tech-savvy and sent the scammer a Grabify link, you might have been able to figure out, loosely, where they are located, as well as the person's IP address. But that's not enough to be able to identify the person and turn them in to authorities.

Be cautious when sharing personal information because you might not really know who you're dealing with. If the person is making you an offer that seems too good to be true, the best course of action is to share no information at all. That free car doesn't exist, and has more strings attached than you even realize (Tekkit Realm, 2022).

Compromised Debit Card Scam

You receive an automated call from your bank, letting you know your debit card has been compromised.

Before you can cancel the card and have another one reissued to you, you must follow the automated prompts, starting with entering your debit card number.

Over the course of this automated process, you'll be asked to verify your debit card number, expiration date, CVV number, full name as it appears on your card, and billing address.

But though it may sound legitimate at first, this is a scam. At no point during the call does the automated message say your name or indicate the call is for you. And at no point does it say the name of the financial institution that issued your debit card. And in rare cases, it might say Bank of America or Chase Bank, but do you have an account with any of those banks?

Everything in the automated message is vague, but if you're in the right state of mind for this scam to work, you'll end up giving away more than enough details for the scammers behind the message to swipe your debit card as they please.

Unfortunately, if your debit card wasn't compromised before, it's definitely compromised now.

It's not enough to say that if you receive a phone call from someone claiming to be a representative from your financial institution, you should just hang up the phone because sometimes, banks do call their customers.

I utilize a national bank for a few of my accounts. And one day, when I returned from a business trip, I received a phone call from a number I didn't recognize. I didn't pick up the phone because I assumed if it was a legitimate call, the person would leave a voicemail, and she did.

But I didn't trust the voicemail either, so I Googled the number and found many people reported the number as legitimate. So, I called my card company directly and confirmed that the call was real and that my card had been compromised.

Since then, without me opting in to receive additional security, this bank has called and texted me to verify potentially fraudulent purchases and other activities.

I'm not sure how common this is with other financial institutions, but I recount this story because it's a testament to the fact that some calls claiming to be from financial institutions are 100% legitimate.

However, be wary of the fact that fake calls are floating around. If the caller or automated prompt doesn't identify which financial institution they belong to and prove the message is specifically intended for you, it's probably a scam.

If you get a call from a live person, in which they ask you to verify your information first, before they tell you any real details about the reason for the phone call, be especially suspicious and don't share any personally identifiable information.

If they are calling you, especially if they claim to be working on behalf of your financial institution, the person should know who you are and be willing and able to prove it.

A scammer pretending to be your bank will tell you that you have to verify your information first, for security reasons, but this is just a cover up for the fact that they don't actually know much about you other than what is publicly available.

If a person cannot verify that they actually work for your bank, or if you are unsure of whether the phone call is legit or not, always hang up and call the phone number listed on the back of your card.

BENEFICIARY SCAM

You receive communication from someone who claims to be a distant relative, or a complete stranger who has identified you as their beneficiary. The person is dying soon and wants to make sure you're all set up to receive the millions of dollars they would like to bequeath to you.

We may not always be aware of all the family members we have, especially if they're extended family, so it's not out of the ordinary for someone who you didn't know you were related to reach out and attempt to make a connection. There are TV shows dedicated to helping people connect with lost family members, in fact.

However, be wary when someone reaches out to you to give you a large sum of money. And be especially wary if, in order to claim this large sum of money, you must share your banking details, sensitive personal information, and/or pay a fee to unlock the funds.

If you really are to receive money, there shouldn't be any monetary strings attached. If the gift was a multi-million-dollar gift, the person giving you the gift should be well-off enough to cover whatever fees might be involved in getting the money into your hands.

Many of us want to receive a life-changing sum of money, but don't let that dream lead you into a nightmare. Be wary of strangers offering you money because few things in life are truly free.

To expose a beneficiary scammer, ask them for details on how this person came to know about you and decide you're worthy of such a generous gift. Ask the scammer how they got your contact information. Ask the scammer details about you. Do they even know your name?

A beneficiary scammer wants you to get so wrapped up in the idea of being a millionaire that you'll do whatever they tell you to do so you can get that money.

But after you send the requested fee along with your personal information, you receive nothing, at best. At worst, your money is stolen, and your identity has been duplicated and sold to people who can now commit crimes pretending to be you (Meskauskas, 2022).

UNEMPLOYMENT BENEFITS SCAM

You recently lost your job.

2020 was the start of a global pandemic. COVID-19 disrupted industries and closed many businesses down for good. Even two years later, the effects are still there. If you lost your job during the pandemic, you may have been entitled to many kinds of benefits.

Additionally, if you were laid-off or fired and you paid unemployment tax out of your wages, you would also be entitled to tap into those benefits. These things, even in combination, may not be enough to sustain you. But in a time where many things were stripped from many people, it's nice to have something to rely on, no matter how unsubstantial.

In vulnerable times like these, watch out for unemployment benefits scams.

Scammers know scamming is a numbers game. And by very obvious calculations, it's safe to say many people are entitled to unemployment benefits due to the increase in unemployed people. If you fit into that bucket, these scammers are relying on you to be in a financial position where you could really use some money now.

Be wary of general and unsolicited communications claiming to help you access your unemployment benefits. I received an email claiming I had unemployment benefits owed to me. To claim them, I just needed to click the link in the email to navigate to a secure form to fill out to get the process started. Because I was fortunate to not have become unemployed during the pandemic, it was very easy for me to spot this as a scam. But if you were or currently are unemployed, this may have seemed like a legitimate communication at first.

If you are entitled to unemployment benefits, know that if you are to receive any communication at all about your benefits, you would receive mail, unless you filled out an application online and opted in to receive email communication. But even then, you will still receive mail regarding your application process.

Most importantly, the communication would be personalized in such a way that you knew it was for you. The email I received didn't even have my name in it. It was just a generic email that could be sent to many people.

If I clicked on the link in that email, I would've been taken to a shady website and asked to put in personal information that could make it very easy for scammers to steal and/or sell my identity. Otherwise, clicking the link could have initiated the download of malicious software that could steal information from my computer as well as render it unusable.

While it may seem harmless to click a link to get more information, know that clicking the wrong link can have serious implications. If the email doesn't have any information indicating it's specifically for you and the email address that sent the email does not look like it belongs to a government entity or past employer, mark the email as spam and delete it.

If you are unemployed and you happen to be waiting for unemployment benefits, you might be an easy target for this scam. Vet the communication you receive regarding your benefits to ensure it's tailored to you and originated from a legitimate email address.

If you receive communication about benefits, but you're unsure if the communication is legitimate, call the entity in charge of the benefits you're requesting to confirm with someone there. If the communication did not originate from that entity and it's not an official communication, they will let you know (Chivers, 2020).

CASH APP/VENMO PAYMENT RECEIPT SCAM

You receive an email from what seems to be Cash App or Venmo, claiming $500 has been deposited into your account. It doesn't say from who, or for what. To find that information, you'll need to click the link in the body of the email.

Except, this isn't how Cash App or Venmo works. Yes, they do send automated emails for certain transactions. However, you would also have received some sort of notification from the app on your phone as well. But even if you turned off notifications, don't bother clicking on the link in the email. Instead, check the app on your phone to see if the deposit is recorded in your account. If that deposit was real, you'd see it in your transaction history. If the deposit was faked to get you to act on the scam email, then you won't see it in the app.

These emails also tend to specify that you have to click the link to accept the $500 deposit, otherwise it won't go through. But this also isn't how Venmo and Cash App work. If you must accept a payment, it won't be via a link in an email. It would have to happen within the app.

Scammers hope you cast judgment aside and act fast. They hope you'll see the hundreds of dollars they claim was sent to you and impulsively click the link out of excitement. But once you do that, you may end up downloading malware onto your computer without even noticing. Once that malware is on your computer, scammers can see a lot of what you're doing online, including when you log into your bank account.

The chances of receiving money out-of-the-blue in a way where you must act now to receive it are slim to none. In fact, you're most likely to lose money when acting on a scam like this. The malware you end up downloading may expose your login information and passwords, making it easy for scammers to log into your online bank and transfer money to their accounts before you even realize the money is missing.

If you lose money from or access to your account, you might be out of luck. Zelle, another peer-to-peer payment app, recently said it's not responsible for money lost to scams through the Zelle app and they have no way to refund money once sent (Yahoo, 2022).

In an instance like this where you receive a communication that claims to be from Cash App or Venmo, the best course of action is to go straight to the app to confirm if the communication is real.

If money was sent to you or requested by you, the app transaction ledger will let you know. Don't click on strange links embedded in unsolicited emails, especially if the emails hold the promise of free money.

PAYPAL SCAMS

While there are multiple scams that can come to you in the name of PayPal, these are the most common ones I've seen:

YOU RECEIVED MONEY SCAM

Like the Cash App and Venmo versions, this one involves scammers sending you an email, claiming to be PayPal, saying you've received a large amount of money. But of course, the email is not legitimate.

Like with most other email scams, when you look at the email address that sent you the email, you'll see discrepancies.

Though the portion of the email address before the "@" symbol may say "PayPal" or "paypalsupport," it's the part after the "@" symbol that actually matters.

Here's an example: You might receive an email from PayPal_support@gmail.com.

The "PayPal_support" portion sounds legitimate. Most companies have an email address that customers can send support requests to. But look at what's after the "@" symbol: gmail.com. PayPal does not utilize gmail.com for official communication because PayPal has its own domain. If you receive an email from PayPal, it will come from @paypal.com, not paypal.net, not paypal.biz, and most certainly not Gmail, Yahoo, or Hotmail.

Scammers are hoping you'll see the amount of money they claim was sent to you and get greedy. They're also hoping you'll see that the portion of the email address before the "@" symbol says "PayPal" and you'll immediately trust that the communication is legitimate.

Any time you receive emails from an organization, look at the half of the email address after the "@" symbol and confirm whether that matches the website of the organization that the email claims to have originated from. In the case of a scam message, that email address will usually not line up with the website address that belongs to the organization the scammer claims they are part of.

And in cases like this, you can be 100% sure it's a scam.

UNAUTHORIZED PURCHASE SCAM

If scammers can't get you to submit to their scams by appealing to greed or desperation, they'll try to get you by way of fear.

It's always scary and frustrating when a financial account is compromised. We keep enough of our money and securities in these accounts that if they become compromised and all funds are drained, we might end up with little to nothing to live on.

What if we can't get any of that stolen money back? What do we do then?

How long will the cash you have in your wallet last if you have no additional access to money?

You can imagine how scary it could be for some to receive an email stating someone has access to their PayPal account and is making purchases with it.

This is the second major way PayPal scammers trick people into giving them money and access to their PayPal accounts. PayPal scammers send out receipts they hope you'll believe are from your actual PayPal account. Or they'll call or email you stating someone tried to make an unauthorized purchase from your PayPal account.

Again, none of this communication is legitimate. If you don't have a PayPal account, you'll quickly realize that someone calling to tell you your PayPal account has been compromised is full of it.

But if you have a PayPal account and this sounds like something you might believe, pause before reacting. Scammers are hoping you'll be spooked enough to act fast. Before you even consider responding, log into your PayPal account (but NOT using any links from the email you received) and check for any activity that doesn't look like it's yours.

Do not click on any links from a potentially fraudulent email. If you're talking on the phone with someone who claims to be from PayPal, do not click on any links they may send to you or read out any PIN numbers you may receive via text message.

Under the guise of pretending to secure your account, PayPal scammers will try to reset your password so they can lock you out of it. To do this, they'll have you click on "Forgot Password" on the PayPal website, which will prompt PayPal to send you a code and/or reset link.

Once scammers get that information, they'll change your password and not tell you what they changed it to. From there, they can either drain your account or hold it for ransom, forcing you to pay a fee to get access to your own account.

When in doubt, don't communicate with anyone who reaches out to you, unprompted, claiming to be from PayPal. Don't respond and don't click on any links.

As with other scam emails, look at the portion after the "@" symbol. In doing this, you'll find that the communication didn't originate from PayPal.com. Clicking any links in the fake scam email could result in compromising your computer and any login and password information you may have stored on your computer.

Instead, go straight to the PayPal website, check your account, then contact support via the PayPal website if you're still unsure.

Amazon Unauthorized Purchase Scam

You receive an email or phone call from someone representing Amazon, which isn't known for contacting people without some obvious reason.

When you answer the phone or read the email, they tell you that someone has made an unauthorized purchase using your account. You are then asked to verify your personal information so the representative can confirm they're talking to the right person.

Once your information is "confirmed," you receive additional information about this unauthorized purchase, including the name of the person who did it, the item they ordered, and the location they're sending that item to.

But don't worry. This representative can help you dispute this charge, they just need to connect to your computer or phone to be able to do this.

Here's the problem: there was no charge.

Unfortunately, there are multiple places within the scam that can cause you problems if you fall for it.

If you let the scammer connect to your computer, they can access whatever stored information, pictures, documents, and passwords you have saved on it.

Additionally, these scammers will try to get you to reset your password. Once they do this, you'll receive a code from Amazon via text or email. The scammer will ask you to read this code to them. But if you do that, they can reset your password, lock you out, and access all the stored personal and financial information in your Amazon account. With this information, they'll often drain the accounts linked to your Amazon account by purchasing gift cards.

You can easily debunk this scam by checking your order history to confirm whether or not the order they claim was placed was actually placed. But the scammer will instruct you to not log into your Amazon account. They'll even claim, if you insist, that logging into your Amazon account at this point will compromise your account and, potentially, your whole computer.

But the reason they don't want you to check your account is because no unauthorized purchase was made. And if you figure that out before handing over your money and your account to the scammer, they know you'll hang up the phone and stop responding.

This may seem like a crazy scam to fall for to some people, but with data breaches and cyber security hacks happening all the time, it's easy to see how someone could think their account has been compromised and forgo the process of vetting the person they're talking to in order to get a quick resolution (TMJ4, 2020).

Refund Scam

In February of last year, you purchased our software. We are discontinuing the service and we're no longer offering support because we're going out of business.

Would you like to cancel your subscription and receive a refund?

When you receive an unexpected communication like this, many questions should come to mind, including:

What product/service is this?

What company is calling me?

What was the exact date that I purchased the product and what is it called?

The caller hasn't addressed me by name. Do they actually know who I am?

You can try asking these questions to a refund scammer, but they will be quick to deflect them. Unfortunately, many people don't bother asking questions at all, which is what refund scammers count on. They're hoping you could really use the money they're offering to you, so you'll be willing to do whatever they tell you to get it.

A refund scam works like this: A scammer will call you and tell you that you have software or a service running on your computer that their company has provided. They may not tell you the name of the company they claim to be calling on behalf of, but they'll be sure to let you know this is a legitimate call made on behalf of a legitimate company to a legitimate customer (i.e., you).

For whatever reason, you've paid for the subscription, but you won't be able to use it going forward. Sometimes, it's because they claim their company is going out of business.

Sometimes, they claim the software was hacked and may corrupt your computer.

Whatever the case, you paid for something that you now cannot use. So, the scammer offers to remove the software from your computer and issue you a refund. They assure you that this refund money is yours; it's owed to you.

The goal is that, to claim your refund, you will allow the scammer to remote connect to your computer. While they are connected, they will ask you to log into your bank account, though in some cases they claim not to see it.

To process your refund, they may pull up a black screen with white text and instruct you to type in your personal information, as well as the amount of the

44

refund. In other cases, they will show you a demo bank account and they'll claim to process the refund from that account.

Whatever they end up showing you is fake; it doesn't really belong to their bank. They'll not only convince you it's real, but they'll also convince you that something went wrong with the transfer and now they need your help.

The climax of a refund scam is that, in trying to process the transfer, too much money was accidentally sent to you. It could have been that the scammer wants you to believe you typed in too many zeros when filling out the fake refund form. Or the scammer may admit they were the one who made a "mistake". But either way, instead of typing in $300 for the refund, for example, someone accidentally typed in $3,000, and now the banking server has sent the incorrect amount of money to your account.

The scammer will then have you log into your bank account to confirm. Once you're logged in, the scammer will edit the HTML webpage in your banking portal to make it look like your balance increased. But nothing really changed with your account. It just looks like something changed. They may transfer money in between your accounts, and only draw your attention to the account they want you to be looking at as having an increased balance. Either way, the amount of money you had across all your accounts never changed. All your money is still there, and no additional money has been sent to you.

The scammer is hoping you'll see this change in the account they want you to focus on and feel bad enough to run to the store to get gift cards for the scammer so they don't lose their job.

Because you've received extra money that the company couldn't afford to lose, you must send the money back immediately. If you seem reluctant, the scammer may even threaten to take legal action against you in order to get the money back.

Even though the scammer claims to have sent money directly into your account, a reversal of that transaction isn't possible, or so the scammer wants you to believe. They will strongly discourage you from calling your bank to cancel the transaction. They often won't accept a debit card payment to get the money back.

Instead, the scammer will try to convince you that their company only accepts payment in gift cards or cryptocurrency, or they'll ask you to withdraw cash from your bank and send it in a package via postal mail. But in the most common scenario, scammers will ask you to get gift cards as these are easy for scammers to redeem and they leave no real paper trail.

Once you provide the gift card codes, both the scammer and your money vanish. Then, when you finally get a chance to check your bank account balances, you'll find that you didn't receive any money from the scammer to begin with. You actually lost money by buying gift cards and giving the codes to the scammer (Contributor, 2020).

Money Flip Scam

Even the wealthiest of us have probably felt, at one time or another, as if we didn't have enough money to feel secure or successful. In times of desperation, it can be tempting to look for quick and easy solutions to make extra money. Money flip scammers offer an interesting, though nonsensical, solution to this very problem.

The premise of the money flip scam is this: people send money through Western Union all the time. Western Union operates in over 200 countries and territories and serves millions of customers every day, making it a very popular and widely used option for sending money (Western Union, 2022). MoneyGram is another major and popular money transfer service.

But for various reasons, not all the money that gets sent ends up being claimed. It could be because of errors in the sending process. It could be because the receiver forgot to pick up the money. It could be because the receiver's bank no longer partners with Western Union or MoneyGram.

In a case where a transaction cannot be completed, the sender can contact the money transfer service's customer service number to get a refund for the incomplete transaction.

But money flip scammers want you to believe that when these transfers are not picked up or refunded, they have access to the funds and are able to disperse that unclaimed money to people like you and me.

For a small fee, a money flip scammer will try to convince you that they can turn your $300 investment into $600, or maybe even $3,000 using the unclaimed Western Union or MoneyGram funds.

But this is not possible. And even if it was, it would be illegal (Green, 2019).

YOUR FACEBOOK ACCOUNT HAS BEEN HACKED SCAM

Facebook boasts billions of users, though more and more data suggests many of these profiles are fake.

Regardless, many people do use Facebook to share photos and videos, connect with family and friends, explore, and participate in different community events, etc. For a lot of people, Facebook is an important resource for connecting with loved ones. For those people, it can be very scary to find out their account has been hacked. The recovery process isn't always straight-forward, and once hackers get into your account, they can change your password and lock you out of the account.

To capitalize on this fear, scammers send out emails claiming your Facebook account has been hacked. Some go as far as to include the name of the hacker in the emails, but of course it's all fake.

Scammers are hoping you'll see the email and be scared enough to click the links in the email or contact them to recover your account. They're also hoping you'll see the name of the "hacker" and panic because you don't know who that person is. But if you do this, you'll walk right into the scam.

You can tell the email is a scam when it's poorly written, the email sender is not from @facebook.com, and, in many cases, the email was sent to an email address that isn't even associated with your Facebook account.

If you get an email claiming to be from Facebook, letting you know your account is hacked, know it's probably a scam. Even if Facebook did immediately know the name of the person who may have compromised your account, they wouldn't tell you who it was.

Once you click on the links in this scam email, it ensures your Facebook account will be compromised soon, if it wasn't before.

Love Spell Scam

Have you ever loved (or obsessed over) someone so much that you would do anything to get them to love you back? If so, you would be the love spell scammer's ideal target.

Love spell scammers thrive on social media sites like Instagram, YouTube, and Facebook. In fact, the chances are high that you've seen them in a comment section or two if you've ever consumed content having to do with love, dating, courtship, breakups, or any other romance-related subject. They figure, if you're watching romance content, you might be desperate enough to fall for their sales pitch. After all, some say love makes us do crazy things.

In the comment section of a YouTube video about the state of online dating in 2022, for example, a love spell scammer will post a fake testimonial or a fake claim that they can help the person of interest in your life fall madly in love with you by casting a spell on them.

Regardless of whether spellcasting is real or not, what I can guarantee is if you decide to contact a WhatsApp number you find in the comment section of a YouTube video and you get in touch with one of these love spell scammers, they will try to drain you of every dollar you have.

They'll charge you for obscure ingredients.

They'll charge you for labor costs, after all casting a spell can be hard work.

And if you're gullible enough to be falling for it, they'll trap you in a never-ending cycle where the spell didn't work for some reason and now you must pay additional money on top of what you've already paid to troubleshoot the various problems they're having with casting your spell. It won't end until you get fed up and stop sending money.

Unfortunately, it's all for nothing, as the object of your affection won't act any differently toward you as a result of the spell the scammer claims to be casting on your behalf. As long as you remain desperate for love and willing to do whatever it takes, the scammer will continue to charge you more and more money without you seeing any real results.

To some people, this probably sounds absolutely ridiculous.

How could anyone fall for this?

Remember that scams succeed when they can sufficiently exploit a pain point or vulnerability. Some people believe in witchcraft. Others don't. But between those two groups, there's an intersection of people who are so enamored with a person that they will do anything to be with them.

Before you mock those who may fall for something you don't think you'd ever fall for, consider that desperation, at some point or another, has caused many of us to consider options we shouldn't. And if you want or need something badly enough that you're willing to do anything to get it, a scammer is ready, willing, and able to exploit that (Kitboga, 2020).

Tech Support Scam

No scam is good.

But if there's anything positive I would say about any scam, I'd say it about this one. This scam at least offers some benefits to victims who are on the receiving end of it.

In a tech support scam, a scammer will try to convince you that something is wrong with your computer. The diagnosis is often fake, but they make it sound real enough to make you consider paying them a fee to fix it.

If you pay, some tech support scammers will sometimes actually do things to your computer that may speed it up and/or make it work slightly better. But the ones who go this extra mile aren't really doing anything that will greatly improve the way your computer functions.

In a tech support scam, a scammer will call you and use some made up storyline to get you to grant them remote access to your computer. When you let the scammer onto your computer, the scammer will run fake commands and deploy fake messages in order to convince you that your computer has a virus and/or that there are hackers on your computer.

For a small fee of anywhere from a few hundred dollars up to a few thousand dollars, a tech support scammer will fix your computer, remove the viruses, and remove all the hackers. Whether there are actually viruses or hackers on your computer is irrelevant here because the scammer usually won't run a real security scan to check for issues.

Instead, they'll run commands on your computer that a regular computer user may not have seen before and try to convince you of their fake diagnoses. They're hoping your fear of viruses and hackers will be great enough that you're willing to hear them out and pay the fee to solve the problems they have identified.

But know this: the things they show you and claim are viruses or hackers are nothing more than basic programming commands that don't mean anything close to what they're trying to convince you they mean. But since these aren't commands the average computer user runs, scammers are hoping you'll blindly trust the process, since you don't know what's going on. Nothing tech support scammers show you is ever indicative of the presence of any virus, malware, or hacker.

If you agree to pay the fees to fix your computer that doesn't actually require any fixing, the scammer may, out of the kindness of their heart, do a few things to clean up your computer. They may clear cookies and cache from your Internet browser, which could reduce some glitches you may have experienced on some websites. They may empty your recycle bin for you. They may even run CCleaner, which cleans up any unused and potentially useless files that may be lingering on your computer from past activity.

All these things can help make your computer work a little bit better. But none of these things have much to do with viruses or hackers, and none of these activities justify the security installation and firewall-restoring work the scammer claims to be doing for you.

Tech support scammers make claims they cannot back up. In fact, among the package options they provide you is often a lifetime plan. It protects your computer over the course of a lifetime, so no viruses or hackers will ever infect your computer again. But these are fly-by-night companies that are aimed at making quick money and then vanishing before they get caught. If you run into an issue on your computer and try to call the tech support scammer back 24-48 hours later, you'll often find the number is out of service.

Once the scammer disappears, what happens to your lifetime service plan? Nothing, because it never existed in the first place. Your computer is just as vulnerable to issues down the line as it was the day the scammer got in contact with you, but potentially more vulnerable if the scammer decided to break your computer after taking your money.

Potentially worse than paying for lifetime support that doesn't actually exist and sending your money to scammers who have nothing beneficial to offer you is the fact that once the scammer gets remote access to your computer, they now have access to all your saved passwords, including banking details, should they decide to look for that information.

In many cases, these scammers search your computer for as much information as they can get. They're liable to do anything, including adding their bank account as a recipient address within your account so they can wire money to themselves without having to go through you to get it. Aside from that, a scammer accessing your personal information also leaves you vulnerable to identity theft.

As a rule of thumb, if someone contacts you out of the blue, regardless of whether they are a tech support scammer or not, if that person asks for remote access to your computer, it's best to decline and hang up the phone because once they get onto your computer, there's not much you can do to stop them from gaining access to everything you have saved to your computer. Unless you're quick to shut down your computer and you're able to uninstall the remote access program they made you install before they get a chance to do anything, and even that is unlikely.

Keep in mind that some scammers, if you catch them in the act after they've connected to your computer, may download malware and viruses onto your computer out of spite if they weren't able to get money from you.

This is why not allowing a scammer onto your computer in the first place protects you from anything the tech support scammer may try to do to you or your computer, including retribution (Microsoft, 2022).

Roku Scam

As mentioned before, scammers buy website URLs that look similar to the major, legitimate websites we recognize in the hopes that you'll type something incorrectly and end up on their site, but not notice.

For example, you've probably heard of Amazon.com. But scammers might buy the website domains Amazon.net and/or Amazn.com. They look similar, but these are not the same website.

Amazon.com is the official website; the other ones are completely unaffiliated with Amazon.

Unfortunately, scammers are using other tactics besides hoping you'll mistype something to get more victims.

Those who are not Internet- and/or marketing-savvy may not have heard of Search Engine Optimization, or SEO. But many scammers are getting really good at using it to trick innocent victims.

SEO is relatively complex in its execution and has a lot of different components and requirements to implement it effectively. This depends a lot on how well the competition is doing, as that affects how much extra effort a website will need to put in to beat them in the rankings.

But to simplify, you can think of SEO as the thing that determines where a website appears on a page of search results. When you search something via Google, SEO is what website owners implement to make their websites show up on the first page, as high as possible, in your search results.

People put in work on their websites and, in many cases, hire consultants so they can get their content listed as high up in the search results of Google, Bing, Yahoo, etc. as possible. That way, when you search for something, you find their content first.

Scammers know SEO can bring victims to them, so they're starting to invest time and money into getting it right. To do this, scammers will pick a particular type of scam they want to run, figure out what search terms they want to optimize their website for, and get to work making their illegitimate websites rise to the top of the results.

The Roku scam is one example of how scammers use SEO to source victims. Roku is a device and service that enables people to access streaming content at a reduced cost. Some TVs have Roku built in. Otherwise, you can buy a standalone Roku device for your TV.

Like any device, a Roku can experience technical issues that require troubleshooting. If you can't troubleshoot the device on your own, you may look for a Roku support number to call, or an online Roku customer support chat to interact with. Unfortunately, Roku scammers implement SEO so well, their sites often rank on the first page of Google. If you pick a random site that you see on the first page of a "Roku tech support" search, you may end up directly calling a scammer.

Unfortunately, there isn't much you can do to determine whether a tech support website is a scam or not until you're actually on the phone with someone from the company and you recognize parts of their script that sound questionable, at best.

This scam pretty closely mirrors the general tech support scam, except the focus here is on your Roku device, not your computer.

But the Roku support scammer will still insist on getting remote access to your computer to help troubleshoot your device. From there, the scammer will insist that your Roku device isn't working because there are hackers and/or viruses on your network.

Of course, that's not true, and this is a scam.

There's nothing wrong with your network. And if you send the scammer Bitcoin or gift card codes as payment, per their request, the scammer will leave you high and dry, with less money in your bank account and a still-dysfunctional Roku device (Kitboga, 2018).

Pyramid Schemes

We hear this phrase a lot, but what is a pyramid scheme?

A pyramid scheme is a system that requires the recruitment of new people in order to generate income for the people who entered into the system the earliest.

It's often referred to as a pyramid because the person at the top makes their money off the backs of the people at the bottom of the structure. To make money, people must recruit people to work underneath them on their teams. For those new recruits to make money, they must recruit people underneath them, and so on, and so on. This recruiting and compensation structure resembles the structure of a pyramid, hence the pyramid scheme terminology.

When we hear the phrase pyramid scheme, we often think of Amway. But it's important to understand that pyramid schemes are still alive and well today. One pyramid scheme going around right now is the Blessing Loom.

With the Blessing Loom, you must recruit people into your group, or Loom, and each person must put in a certain dollar amount, often $100. Everyone puts in money for a chance to be one of the lucky winners who receive more money than they put in. Most of the people in the Loom won't receive a penny, regardless of what they put in.

True to its pyramid scheme nature, for the new members of the Loom to get a chance at making anything, they have to bring in new people. And those new people will also get nothing unless they bring in new people. $100 is a lot to lose for some to put in a pot that you know you'll get nothing from. But scammers are hoping you'll be so amazed by the amount they make from bringing people into their Loom that you don't realize you're guaranteed to lose upfront unless you quickly recruit other people who are willing to lose upfront.

And while I explicitly mention the Blessing Loom, this is not the only one that's going around.

To spot a pyramid scheme, look for something disguised as an opportunity to make money that requires you to:

1. Pay into the system, **and**
2. Recruit people underneath you in order to make any sort of financial gain.

If you must pay to enter the system and not recruiting enough people underneath you causes you to not make, or even lose, money, this is a big red flag.

Many people lump all Multi-Level Marketing (MLM) companies into the pyramid scheme category because they do share certain characteristics in common. However, MLMs are not traditional pyramid schemes because, while they do have a heavy emphasis on recruiting other people in order to increase the amount of income that representatives can make, MLM companies today now also offer products and services, which excludes them from being *traditional* pyramid schemes.

That said, it is worth mentioning that if you have been the recipient of predatory behavior by an MLM representative or someone you know has been taken advantage of by an MLM representative or company, you can and should feel empowered to report this to the FTC (Gov, 2022).

IRS/CRA/HMRC Scams

Scammers know they can run the same scams in the US, Canada, UK, and Australia if they slightly edit their scripts.

In scams where the scammer pretends to work for the government, they simply swap out "Social Security Administration" for "HMRC" or "Canada Revenue Agency" or any other government agency to convince a potential victim of their legitimacy.

Even though the agencies and target market are different, this game is exactly the same.

Claiming to work on behalf of these government agencies, scammers will run one of the following two scams:

ILLEGAL ACTIVITY/STOLEN SSN

For this scam, someone will call you to let you know that your social security number (if you're in the US), social insurance number (if you're in Canada), etc. has been flagged for suspicious activity. The fake scenario is that your social number was used to rent a car that was used for illegal activity. The illegal activity tends to involve cocaine and/or other narcotics. If you're in the US, all this activity seems to have happened in the state of Texas.

But if any of this was true, you would probably have law enforcement officers banging down your door by now. If not, you would have at least received a letter in the mail instead of a random phone call. In the United States, the Social Security Administration does not contact people by phone; all official correspondence is done by mail.

More scammers know this now, so they build a line into their scripts explaining that they attempted to send a letter to your home address, but you never responded to it, or it was returned to them. Unfortunately, this makes the scam sound more believable because yes, sometimes mail does go missing.

This, in combination with the fact that scammers now have access to your name and physical address thanks to public records, makes it much easier for scammers to trick people into thinking they really are calling on behalf of the government.

The scammer, then, spends time trying to get you to believe they are federal enforcement officers who must now investigate this case and help you prove your innocence, unless you really were the person who committed the illegal activities registered to your social number. Once they have convinced you that they are who they claim to be, they'll ask about your bank accounts. They claim the illegal activity under your social includes several bank accounts, so they'll ask you to confirm which banks you use and what balances you carry in each.

Then, they take it a step further. The scammer will tell you that you need to withdraw the money from all your accounts and load it onto secure government vouchers until they are able to determine which bank accounts are yours and which ones registered under your name are being used for money laundering.

Those government vouchers that you have to put all your money on are nothing more than store gift cards. Gift cards are NOT government vouchers, but the scammer wants you to believe they are. Once you put all your money on the gift cards and share the codes with the scammer, your money will be stolen.

The scammer will claim that once your identity is cleared and your new social number is issued, you'll receive all your money back. None of this is true, and once you send your money, it's gone.

If you choose not to follow their plan for resolving this matter, the scammer will threaten legal action in the form of imprisonment, as well as a large monetary fine.

But it's all a bluff.

The easiest things to look out for to spot this scam are instances during the conversation in which it's clear to see that the scammer doesn't actually know anything about you other than what's publicly available. The scammer may have your address, birthday/age, and phone number, but they do not actually have your social security number. If the scammer asks you to confirm the number or the last four digits of your social security number, know that you're most likely being targeted by a scam.

There is no Toyota Camry full of 22 pounds worth of cocaine that is tied to your social security or social insurance number.

The government would never call you and ask you to confirm incredibly sensitive information.

The government would also never charge you via gift cards or cryptocurrency to have a new social security number issued to you.

Tax Evasion Scam

Another common IRS, CRA, HMRC, etc. scam revolves around tax evasion.

For this scam, the caller will try to convince you that you accidentally filed your taxes incorrectly. Over the course of the call, however, they accuse you of doing it on purpose to defraud the government and avoid paying taxes.

In many scripts I've seen and heard for this scam, the dates you are given for this alleged fraud span from 2008 to 2012. But the dates are made up and purposely from years ago to make it sound more believable and official.

Often, tax evasion scammers will ask if you filed the taxes yourself, or if you hired someone to file them for you.

But there's no right answer to this question.

If you filed your taxes yourself, the scammer will either spin it as you defrauded the government on purpose or suggest you must have made an honest mistake because tax forms are long and complicated, especially for those who aren't professional tax filers.

If you say you hired a third party to file your taxes for you, the scammer will spin it as the third party must have not known what they were doing, or the scammer will try to convince you that the third party you hired was not authorized to file taxes for you. By hiring a third party, you are now completely liable for that third party's mistakes.

None of this is valid. The government would have sent you a letter outlining these issues for you if there were, indeed, issues found. And in some cases, for certain minor mistakes, your tax forms may be automatically corrected. This has happened to me.

Some of these scammers know this, so they include language in their script to explain that a letter was sent, you just didn't receive it or didn't respond. And though that might sound somewhat believable, there are issues with the rest of the script for this scam.

Most notably, if you wish to resolve this tax evasion matter, you must pay a fine in gift cards or Bitcoin. While I can't speak for other countries that have been quicker to adopt cryptocurrency as a payment option,

I can say that the US and Canadian governments, where this scam tends to be the most popular, would never ask you to pay exclusively by these means.

And though retailers in these two countries are now starting to accept cryptocurrency at their own discretion, neither of the governments in these countries are at a point where they are accepting cryptocurrency as your only means of payment. Down the line, crypto may be **an** option. But scammers will claim crypto and gift cards are your **only** options.

The scammer will never tell you which form you filled out. Different marital statuses and employment statuses require different forms, but the scammer doesn't really know who you are, so they have no access to what forms you filed to confirm that information. And don't even try to ask where on the tax forms you made the mistake.

Was it line 58 on the 1040 EZ?

Was it on your Schedule C?

The scammer has no idea because they don't actually work for the government.

Tax evasion scammers are hoping they can scare you enough to believe you're really in trouble with the government. A fear of being in trouble with the government may get someone to act and comply with a scam they otherwise may not have fallen for if it was related to something less serious (Gov, 2022).

IMMIGRATION SCAM

For many immigrants, the thought of deportation may seem like a nightmare. After working so hard to acquire and maintain citizenship over the course of several years - building a career, fostering personal and professional connections, and creating a home and life for oneself, the thought of being deported and having to start all over sounds not only inconvenient, but almost impossible.

Thus, many immigrants go above and beyond to stay in compliance with all government rules and up to date with all citizenship paperwork. Unfortunately, this desire to stay in the country of their choosing makes immigrants extremely vulnerable to immigration-related scams.

Though the immigration scam can take on multiple different forms, the version I'm most familiar with is a phone call stating that the call recipient's documentation is incomplete and now they must pay a fine of several thousand dollars in order to avoid deportation.

Many versions of this call exist in different languages. If you've received a communication in a language you didn't explicitly request communication in, especially from a phone number you are unfamiliar with, it might have been some iteration of the immigration scam (Hebert et al., 2022).

DEA/POLICE SCAM

No one wants to get in trouble with the law, and scammers know this. That's why most scare tactics for the scams I've mentioned center around threatening legal penalties/actions.

But this scam takes it several steps further because scammers who run these types of scams claim they work for law enforcement, and they already have a warrant out for your arrest.

If you ask what you did, they'll give you some sort of bogus monologue about the crimes they've found linked to your name, but it's all fake.

DEA/Police scammers tend to request several thousands of dollars in fees to cancel your warrant, but law enforcement will never, ever call you threatening to arrest you if you don't pay via Western Union or MoneyGram (The Hoax Hotel, 2015).

If anything, if there really was an arrest warrant out for you, law enforcement would show up to your door instead of calling you and tipping you off.

But once DEA/Police scammers have you on the phone, they work hard to convince you they're legit. They tell you that law enforcement officers know where you are, and they will immediately move in to arrest you if you hang up on them. For many, that is terrifying.

Like other scammers, they urge you not to inform the Western Union or MoneyGram clerk of what's going on. This is because if you tell the clerk you're sending money to the DEA, they'll tell you it's a scam and the scammer will be out several thousand dollars (DEA, 2021).

ILLEGAL PACKAGE - US CUSTOMS & BORDER PATROL SCAM

I was a third of the way through writing my first draft of this book when I received this scam call. Prior to this, I never knew this scam was making its rounds.

This scam takes on a similar profile as the IRS/CRA scam involving illegal activity linked to a car with cocaine in it near the south border of Texas. However, the difference with this scam is these scammers pretend to be from US Customs & Border Patrol.

Instead of your name and social security number being linked to an abandoned car in Texas with drug residue inside it, your information is linked to a package containing illegal substances in it that was intercepted on its way to Texas.

There is no illegal package from Mexico en route to Texas with drugs in it linked to your name and social security number.

Unless there is.

But even if so, if you got caught, you probably wouldn't have a US Marshal from Texas calling you about it. You're more likely to have FBI agents show up at your door unannounced than to receive a cold call about any illegal activity you might be up to.

It feels worth mentioning (again) that I like to waste scammers' time by picking up the phone and pretending to fall for whatever they're telling me. I'm normally not able to keep them on the phone longer than 10-15 minutes, but with this scam, I reached a new personal record. I kept the scammers from the US Customs and Border Patrol occupied for 1 hour, 13 minutes, and 43 seconds.

GOVERNMENT GRANT SCAM

You receive communication via email or phone call from the government offering you a multi-thousand-dollar or, in some cases, multi-million-dollar grant that you can use as you please.

It doesn't matter whether you're a student, a business owner, or any other circumstance. The government wants to give you this money free and clear to use as you please, with a few exceptions being that you can't use it for drugs, gambling, or anything else the scammers claim is illegal in your country.

It's interesting that they put that part in the script to say you can't use the money for gambling or alcohol because those are not illegal in the United States, where this scam is very commonly executed.

If you weren't thrown off by the government calling you from a number that's not associated with the government and offering you thousands or millions of dollars for no reason, you might have been thrown off by this part of the script being inaccurate.

But as with other scam communications, there will always be discrepancies.

If you weren't thrown off by the government contacting you out of the blue to give you free money, or by the fact that a supposed government official is telling you alcohol and gambling are illegal in your country when they are not, the processes you must go through in order to receive your funds might send off the alarm bells.

It's often said that if you have to pay money to receive things that are marketed as free, it's probably a scam, and this is no different. In order for you to receive your free multi-thousand dollar or multi-million-dollar grant, you have to pay a fee in the form of gift cards or cryptocurrency.

Not only do governments not accept payment in gift cards or cryptocurrency, but it's always interesting when someone offers a large sum of money but charges a fee that, in theory, could be covered many times over by reducing it from the grant money.

Why wouldn't they just withhold that fee from the grant money as a tax, so you don't have to pay anything?

The scammer will tell you that's simply not how it works, without further explanation. But the real explanation is it's a scam and there is no grant in the first place (Mikkelson, 2004).

Forex/Stock Investing Scams

Investment-related scams are very common on YouTube, Instagram, and other social media sites. If you consume finance content, you've definitely seen evidence of them.

What do they look like?

You're watching a video about investing tips to build that generational wealth everyone keeps talking about. And as you scroll through the comments on the video to find confirmation that the information in the video is legitimate, you see people posting success stories.

But the success stories have nothing to do with what's being talked about in the video. Instead, these unrelated comments claim some unrelated investment portfolio manager helped them make hundreds of thousands, if not millions, of dollars with their investing strategies.

You'd like to be making hundreds of thousands, if not millions, of dollars with their proven investment strategies, too. So, you're intrigued.

But if you contact the WhatsApp number or email address provided, you'll end up contacting a scammer who might have proven investing strategies, but they won't use those for you.

There are real people behind these fake accounts who want to convince you to "invest" your money with them. But if you send your money to these scammers to invest for you, they'll just end up stealing it.

You may not even find that out until you try to cash out your money.

These scammers are in it for the long-haul. They want you to keep sending money, so they fabricate screenshots and build fake dashboards that show massive returns on your investment to make you think you're earning money. As you see your investment grow, you become willing to send even more money. You might even cash out your investments elsewhere and add them to the amount the scammer is pretending to have invested for you.

And once you send your money over to these fake investors, it's gone forever (Australian Competition and Consumer Commission, 2021).

CRYPTOCURRENCY SCAMS

There are many types of scams that plague the cryptocurrency market, and they can be very hard to detect, especially in a world where everyone is looking for the next best thing, the next Bitcoin, the next 1000x opportunity, the quickest road to millions.

But with cryptocurrency, sometimes it can be difficult to understand what you're buying. Anyone with enough technical knowledge can create a new coin or token, artificially inflate the price, and convince people to buy while they cash out their gains and leave everyone else with losses.

This practice is known as a pump-and-dump scheme because the price is pumped by the entities hoping to make a profit and then dumped while they're still in the green.

With any investment, it's wise to do your research before diving in. Don't react on hype alone. And if, in your research, all you find is people explaining that a crypto offering will make you rich without providing any information or pointing you in the direction of information that indicates it has the value to do so, be wary.

Even with ample documentation, it can still be tough to discern what's valuable and what's not.

Also be wary when you see advertising or receive outreach regarding free cryptocurrency. While there are legitimate ways to get your hands on free cryptocurrency, like signing up for promotions and bonuses from reputable crypto exchanges like Coinbase and Nexo, not all free cryptocurrency is actually free. If you're responding to a random text message or comment on a YouTube video or other social media post, you're more likely to end up giving up your personal information and potentially also your money without ever getting any free crypto (Kaspersky, 2022).

Extended Car Warranty Scam

This scam call goes out to almost everyone, regardless of whether you own a car or not.

How it works is a company that rarely identifies itself by name at any point in the beginning of the call reaches out to you to let you know that your car warranty is close to expiring, if it hasn't expired already. This company wants to offer you extended warranty coverage so that, in the case of major damage to your vehicle that requires expensive repairs, you'll be covered, and you won't have to pay so much out of pocket.

I bought my car certified pre-owned and my warranty lasted about three years. That was incredible for me to not have to worry about out-of-pocket expenses, especially since this was my first car and I was still a relatively new driver. I'm a big advocate for anything that cuts costs and/or gives peace of mind like my car warranty did for me. With this scam, scammers are hoping you'll feel the same way.

On the surface, extra coverage for something as expensive to upkeep as a car sounds great!

But try asking these scammers if you can get back to them because you want to make sure your car company and preferred service center accept their warranty coverage. When you do that, they tend to get irritated because they want you to buy now.

But keep this in mind: first of all, you don't even know if the warranty is legitimate, especially since the person on the other end of the line is withholding the name of the company that's offering the coverage. When they do tell you who they're calling on behalf of, you research it, and confirm it is a real company. But you'll often find very negative reviews indicating the coverage, in some way, shape, or form, falls short of what was promised.

If you want an extended warranty for your vehicle, it's best to go to your car manufacturer or a nationally recognized and well-reviewed company instead of trying to cut costs and corners by working with a company that won't even tell you who they are over the phone because they know you'll find their awful Better Business Bureau reviews if they do tell you and give you enough space to Google it.

In the event that the extended warranty company that called you is real, then this isn't a traditional scam in that you're spending your money on something that doesn't exist, for a benefit you'll never realize in the end. However, the offerings presented to you from these companies tend to be disingenuous and are often much less helpful or cost-saving than what you can get from your actual car manufacturer (Brennan, 2022).

PET-FOR-SALE SCAM

You're in the market for a new pet, so you Google "Corgis for sale."

You're bombarded with a lot of options for where you can find the pet you want - animal shelters, breeders, pet adoption agencies, etc. that have puppies you can purchase.

You end up clicking on a website that doesn't look all that great, but no red flags jump out at you right away. You pick the dog you want, and you're instructed to contact a representative before you submit payment.

You contact the rep and they let you know the dog you're interested in is still available, which is great! Now all you have to do is send payment via Western Union money transfer, MoneyGram money transfer, gift cards, or cryptocurrency. Once your payment is received, your pet will be delivered right to your doorstep.

Or so they say. But it's not true. There is no pet. And when you send your money to the scammer, you get nothing in return.

With this scam, it's not enough to write off a website that looks poorly built. Some legitimate companies don't have the sleekest looking websites, and some scam operations have incredibly professional looking websites. Aesthetics alone aren't enough to save you from falling for this scam.

But the payment method options should be enough to deter you now that you know how prevalent these methods are among scammers.

Pet scams are abundant, especially during the COVID-19 pandemic, because a lot of people were looking for furry friends to add to their families and help keep them sane and occupied while stuck at home.

But if you are looking to get a pet, consider adopting through a reputable organization that you can find real location information and reviews for.

If you insist on purchasing a purebred pet, make sure to vet the organization you're hoping to buy from by looking for reviews, anecdotes, and evidence that they actually sell what they claim to be selling. If the organization is legitimate, it's also worth going the extra mile to make sure you aren't buying from someone who uses unethical or abusive breeding practices (Green, 2020).

HOUSING SCAM

Housing scammers prey on people who need a place to live, and it works like this:

You're browsing on Trulia, Zillow, or another website that is legit for finding housing options. If you're a student looking for a sublet, you may be browsing on Facebook in a group created specifically for students at the college or university you attend.

Either way, you're looking for housing in a place that is generally trustworthy for finding options.

And as you look through the options, you come across one with a price that is too good to be true. (**Hint:** Because it is too good to be true.)

So, you reach out to find out more information. A scammer, unbeknownst to you, then talks you through what they are pretending is an interview process to get to know you because they want to make sure you'll be a good tenant for the space they're renting. Once they entice you enough, they'll let you know you're approved to move in. All you have to do is fill out the housing application they send you and pay a fee.

The housing application you are asked to fill out makes it look incredibly legit. But it's not. At best, the form is a technicality to make things look real. At worst, by filling out that application, you're handing your identity over to someone who might use it or sell it to someone else.

The scary part is you won't even know in some instances that you're dealing with a housing scammer until you show up at the property you thought you were buying or renting to move in, only to find that either the location doesn't exist, or it wasn't up for sale or rent in the first place.

Housing scammers find pictures of real apartments and houses and list them online in places where they know people are looking for a place to live.

With those real photos, scammers flood completely legitimate sites with listings, and people fall for it all the time. On many home and apartment search sites, people can list their own housing accommodations, even if they're not realtors. Without knowing this, you might assume every listing you see was vetted and approved. But that's not the case.

So, how can you tell you're being targeted by a housing scam?

First and foremost, the price will often be too good to be true. Though some housing scammers are smart enough to request a deposit equal to the first and/or last month's rent, many housing scammers request very small deposits and pretend they're lowering the price to ensure they're renting or selling to a good tenant. If the price seems too low, do a quick search online to see what the type of unit you're looking for typically rents/sells for.

If the price doesn't give off red flags because it is in line with current market prices, the next thing you need to do is ask to go see the unit in person. It's a normal request to want to tour a place before you move in, but housing scammers often don't have a way to successfully host a housing tour.

When you ask to go see the unit, the scammer will often deflect or give you an excuse for why you can't see the unit until after you've paid and are ready to move in. In many cases, they'll tell you they can't walk you through the unit because they're out of the country. This is a huge red flag.

Consider scoping out the listing on other websites to see if it's listed anywhere else. If it's not, that's a sign that the listing might not be real. If you're feeling particularly like a detective, you could try going to the unit and looking for signs the place is not for sale and/or currently very much lived in.

There's another version of the housing scam that's even scarier because it's harder to protect yourself against. For this more advanced iteration, you could be in the process of buying a house - a real house that is on the market, and you're working with a real agent and a real broker. You could be doing all of the right steps to purchase a real home.

However, if you receive a phishing email or someone has compromised the email address of your mortgage broker, a phishing scammer could intercept and edit the email that directs you where to send your initial wire transfer deposit and replace the legitimate bank account associated with that financial institution with their own banking details. If this happens, you wouldn't know until your mortgage company tells you they never received any payment from you. By then, it might be too late to stop the transaction.

It is imperative that while you're in the process of buying a house, you remain exceptionally diligent with all email correspondence that comes to you because if your email address gets hacked, you could be hit with this scam and not even know.

Unfortunately, one couple found all of this out the hard way when they sent a payment to a scammer instead of their mortgage lender.

They had no idea this happened until their mortgage lender followed up to let them know no payment was ever received.

So, what can you do when you identify that you've encountered a housing scam?

Report the listing and continue your search elsewhere (Green, 2019), (Green, 2020).

Your Computer Has Been Hacked/Virus Pop-Up Scam

You type "Amazon.com" into your Internet browser's address bar because you want to buy something on Amazon.

But once you land on what you thought was the Amazon homepage, you get a pop-up.

It covers your whole computer screen. It might even be flashing and scary looking.

There's a phone number listed on the pop-up. If you want to get rid of it, you'll have to call that phone number. Unfortunately, if you do that, you'll walk yourself right into a scam that's very similar to the tech support scam.

The scammer on the other end of the phone will try to remotely connect to your computer and try to convince you that there are hackers and/or viruses they can remove from your computer for you, for a fee, of course.

This is a scam, but to some it may not seem that way at first.

Amazon.com is a reputable website. Bestbuy.com is a reputable website. And if you go to one of those websites, you probably won't get this pop-up.

However, if you mistype Amazon.com as Amazn.com, or in any other way that scammers might have anticipated, and you don't notice your mistake, you could end up on a fake clone website, looking at a fake pop-up.

That's because scammers have discovered common ways people mistype website addresses, so they purchase these website domains and deploy fake messages on them to scare victims into giving them a call.

And if you landed on one of these pages, you might be convinced to call, if for no other reason than the pop-up won't go away.

What can be most frustrating about this particular scam is the pop-ups often don't allow you to use your browser buttons to go back. If you're someone who relies on that "Back" button, you might actually think your computer is stuck the way it is, so you might give in and call the scam phone number.

Many of these pop-ups are also hard to close because they often don't have an "x" button in the top right corner. Or, if they do, the "x" button doesn't work. In a scenario like that where none of the tricks you know to get rid of a pop-up are working, again, you might be inclined to give the scam number on the fake pop-up a call.

But the answer to getting rid of the pop-up is really simple. Instead of trying to close the pop-up, simply close the tab or browser where you're getting the pop-up and open a new one.

Because the fake webpage might not load and the pop-up can block your whole screen, you might not even realize you typed a website URL incorrectly to begin with. Without looking back at the website address bar to confirm you typed in the right URL, you might believe the pop-up is legitimate.

Unfortunately, if you thought it was a legitimate pop-up and you called the number provided to get this fake issue resolved, you could end up paying hundreds, if not thousands, of dollars to scammers who will claim to fix your computer but won't really do much because there's nothing wrong with your computer in the first place.

Another angle of this scam involves scammers downloading software onto your computer so they can deploy this pop-up on your computer whenever they want to try to get more money off you.

If you fell for this scam once and let a scammer remote connect to your computer, they might do this to you so you can be a repeat customer.

Also keep in mind that scammers who run these scams often don't charge one fixed amount for everyone. If they're able to remotely connect to your computer and convince you to log into your bank account while they're watching, even if they claim not to be, the amount of money they see that you have will inform how much they end up charging you.

If you don't login to your bank account in front of the scammer, they might ask you how much you're able to pay, instead of telling you how much it costs.

Unsurprisingly, the more money you have, the more money they will try to convince you to pay.

In some cases, when you leave your computer to be serviced by the scammers, they may actually install some helpful software, delete some unused files that are or could be slowing your computer down, etc. However, there is no virus. There are no hackers. Your computer is not infected, no matter what these fake pop-ups try to tell you. And you don't need any of the services a scammer might provide for you (Browning, 2021).

Lottery Scam

While other scams tend to operate through one medium, lottery scams can either target you via phone call, text message, or email.

Over the phone, a lottery scammer will tell you that you won millions of dollars in a lottery you haven't even heard of because you never entered it in the first place. But sometimes, an offer that sounds too good to be true can also sound too good to pass up.

A lottery scammer may also try to reach you via email with a similar proposition. Still, it's on behalf of a lottery fund you've never heard of because you never entered the competition in the first place.

To claim your prize, the lottery scammer will tell you that you need to send a fee via Western Union before you can receive your prize.

Keep in mind that free money is incredibly hard to come by, especially if it's millions of dollars' worth of free money. And a situation in which someone wants to give you a lot of something in exchange for nothing or very little should be evaluated with caution. There's often more than meets the eye in an uneven exchange.

The lottery fee is only a few hundred dollars, which seems like a drop in the bucket compared to the millions of dollars the scammer claims you'll be receiving soon. In fact, it's such a small fee compared to your winnings that you could just have it taken out of the lottery winnings, the same way a government entity may take taxes out of a paycheck or real lottery win before dispersing your money to you.

But if you ask a lottery scammer to take the fee out of your lottery winnings, they'll tell you they can't do that.

Why?

Because the money the scammer wants you to believe you won doesn't exist. There's no multi-million-dollar fund to take the fee out of. But the scammer is hoping you'll consider the fee a very small price to pay for the winnings you think you'll get, so you'll be willing to give them your money.

In a case like this, there are two things to keep in mind: first, remember that if something sounds too good to be true, it probably is. And second, if you didn't apply for an opportunity but, somehow, that opportunity finds you out of the blue in a way you're unfamiliar with or don't have prior connections to, it's most likely a scam (Lottery, 2022).

You're Today's Winner! Click Here to Claim Your Prize! Scam

You land on a website after conducting a Google search, and you're greeted with a flashing pop-up with some exciting news.

According to the pop-up, you won a monetary prize. It could be $1,000. It could be $100. It could be millions of dollars. Whatever the case, winning a prize just for landing on a website sounds like a great deal.

Unfortunately, this is a scam.

Many people recognize this scam and don't act on it.

However, it is nice to feel like you've won something. Some people will see this pop-up and click the link to try to claim their prize.

In some cases, this pop-up does not lead to a malicious site. Instead, it leads to a page with a lot of affiliate links that prompt you to fill out several forms and pay for shipping fees on products you don't even want before you get your prize.

Whether you get your prize or not depends on the site you end up on.

But in other cases, clicking the link downloads any number of malicious files that can log your passwords and destroy your computer. The best course of action is to close the pop-up and not click on any links within it.

Though some of these pop-ups can take over your whole screen and seem impossible to get rid of, you can close the tab or window to get rid of the pop-up (Meskauskas, 2022).

FREE GIFT CARD SCAM

You've been selected to receive a free $100 gift card or voucher to a store or restaurant of your choosing. All you have to do is answer a brief survey and pay for the cost of shipping the gift card to you. It sounds like a great deal, except it's a scam.

Whether there is a gift card on its way to you after you complete the survey or not is irrelevant. What matters is that, to pay the $4.99 shipping fee, you'll have to give the scammer your full debit card or credit card information - your full name as it appears on the card, the card number, CVV number, etc.

When you authorize the scammer to charge your card the shipping fee, you don't realize that you're authorizing them to sign you up for subscriptions that, after a 14-day free trial lapses, will continue to bill your card until you cancel.

Aside from that, having your card information gives the scammer the opportunity to charge it to its limit.

KIDNAP SCAM

On a random afternoon, you receive a call from someone claiming to be holding your loved one for ransom. If you're especially unlucky, the person on the other end of the line may let you hear the sound of your loved one scream. In that moment, you feel helpless and terrified.

In order to set your loved one free, you'll have to pay ransom. But what do you do if you don't have the money?

What do you do if you send the money via Western Union like the kidnapper asks you to, but they don't release your loved one?

The bad news is, even if you pay the ransom, the kidnapper won't release your loved one.

The good news is the kidnapper never had your loved one captive in the first place.

This incredibly predatory scam puts the life or death of someone you care about in your hands, so it's no wonder people act immediately.

But none of it is real. In fact, if you get a call like this, hang up the phone immediately and contact the loved one who the scammer claims to have kidnapped. Once you get a hold of that person, you'll see it was all an evil, sadistic ruse (Burton, 2021), (NIH, 2022).

TEXT MESSAGE SCAMS

If you receive a text message from a phone number you do not recognize and you did not opt-in to receive that message, the contents of that text could very well be scam-related.

Scammers are getting craftier with how they reach out to people, and text messages are a common and quick medium for communication. We tend to check our text messages without fully processing what we're reading or looking at, and scammers are hoping that when you open their messages, without thinking much of them, you'll click on malicious links.

In this digital world, many of us are opting-in to receive communication from all sorts of different organizations.

We opt-in to receive messages from postal services so we can track our shipments.

We opt-in to receive text messages about employment opportunities, interview scheduling, etc.

We opt-in for workplace communications.

We opt-in for discounts and deals.

We opt-in for updates.

And we don't save any of those numbers to our phones, because why would we? Even if we could, the text messages don't always come from the same numbers.

Text messages from numbers we don't recognize might not be out-of-the-ordinary for you, and that's why you should be extra cautious of text message scams.

There isn't just one type of scam that plagues mobile phones around the world. Text message scams can range from fake job opportunities to messages masquerading as friends or family in need of urgent assistance, so sometimes it can be hard to differentiate a legitimate message from a scam.

Know that if you mistake a scam message for something trustworthy and click on any links or download any files attached to it, you run the risk of exposing your personal information or downloading spyware, malware, or other unwanted applications.

In the Appendix, I'll share a few scam text messages I have personally received. But those are not the only scam text messages floating around. The rule of thumb is to pause and use your best judgment. If it's a message from a phone number you don't recognize or about something you don't remember opting-in to know more about, don't act on the message, at least not right away.

The majority of the scams I discuss in this book, including this one, rely on you acting quickly without taking the time to think it through, so the best thing you can do is give yourself time to evaluate whether or not the message you received seems legitimate to you before you act (Panda Security, 2022).

UPS/FedEx Package Delivery Notification Scam

Since the invention of eBay and Amazon for things other than books, online shopping has only continued to grow and become a lot of people's go-to source for shopping online. Online shopping has become, in many ways, much more accessible than shopping in-store thanks to courier services like UPS, USPS, FedEx, DHL, and other carriers.

Scammers know chances are high that you're currently waiting on a package to be shipped to you. They've turned to generating spam emails masquerading as shipment notifications that your package is either on the way or has been shipped. But if you look closely at the sender addresses for these shipment notices, you'll see they aren't coming from actual courier companies. That's why it's important to look at the email address that's sending you the communication.

However, if you are waiting for a package, it can be easy to move quickly and click the links in the email to get a status on your package.

If you do that, you'll fall right into the trap. By clicking on those links, you could end up downloading malicious software that gives scammers access to all the information stored and saved on whichever device you clicked the links on.

The best way to avoid falling for a scam like this is to look at the email sender information. If the email claims to be from a courier service like DHL or FedEx, make sure the email is being sent from an email address associated with that courier service. If it isn't, disregard the email.

MIRACLE CURES/HEALTH-RELATED SCAMS

Depending on how old you are, you may or may not remember Peter Popoff. I know that name very well because someone very close to me fell for his fraud. I will refrain from providing any information that will identify that person and/or their relation to me, but I will share this person's story because it's very relevant.

Depending on where you live and what time you're watching TV, you might see those late-night infomercials for products and services that tend to be very gimmicky. So gimmicky that you wonder who's buying that stuff, anyway.

But it's important to remember that regardless of age, anyone can be deceived. And while some people are targeting the elderly or immigrants, others are targeting people battling illness.

Enter Peter Popoff.

Peter Popoff was a late-night televangelist and faith healer. On his late-night show and in infomercials, he would pray for people and encouraged viewers to subscribe to his various healing programs so they could be healed from their afflictions like his audience members.

Invoking religion and the name of God, which is enough to hook devoutly religious people, he would promise healing to those who were desperate for a solution. For a price, of course. At the time my loved one discovered Popoff, they were suffering from arthritis. This person's fingers were often incredibly swollen, making everyday activities burdensome at best, and impossible at worst.

On a random night, they flipped through TV channels looking for something to watch and found a religious network. In times of struggle, this person turns to God for support. That night, Peter Popoff happened to be on TV praying for people. That night's segment was timely and relevant as he prayed for someone watching at home who was suffering from joint pain that was inhibiting their daily life. This person felt as though that message was meant just for them.

In reality, a message about someone experiencing joint pain is incredibly generic. Many people suffer from Multiple Sclerosis, arthritis, Lupus, and other physical ailments that make daily life difficult and painful.

Unfortunately, it also hit close to home. My loved one, and many others like them, was desperate for healing, desperate enough to pay whatever it cost to be healed. Peter Popoff sold access to his healing via prayer cards, blessed oils, and other "holy" means. And he made millions every year doing it.

If something sounds too good to be true, it is. Unfortunately, Peter Popoff isn't the only fake healer who made money this way. Others have gone after him to sell their own tinctures and potions that they claim cure cancer, COVID, and various other ailments. As long as people remain suffering and vulnerable, health-related scams will probably continue.

You don't have to be elderly to fall for a scam like this; it's not always about age. Sometimes, the right message delivered to you in a moment of desperation is enough to make you put your better judgment aside.

POWER COMPANY/ELECTRIC BILL SCAM

Electricity powers so much of what those of us who have access to it do. Cell phones, laptops, refrigerators, ovens, microwaves, breathing devices, medical equipment, etc. can only run for so long without eventually being plugged into an electricity source.

That's why power outages can be incredibly inconvenient for some and life-threatening for others.

Unfortunately, some scammers have found out that threatening to cut electricity for some people works.

A power company scammer will call you claiming you have an overdue balance on your electricity bill. If you don't pay in the next few minutes, or hours, your electricity will be cut.

The bad news is these scammers work in specific regions, so they tend to know what electric companies the people they call are using. This can make the call sound legitimate if the scammer correctly names the company you use over the phone.

The good news is these scammers often know nothing else about you aside from what electric company you use.

If someone calling you, claiming to work for your electric company, doesn't know your name and can't confirm your account number with that electric company, you can and should hang up because that phone call is not legitimate (Fox8News, 2018).

Chapter 3. Education & Resources

In this book, you learned about a variety of scams operating today, as well as various methods to help you identify those scams and avoid falling for them.

There are a variety of other resources you can use to learn more about scams, including:

YouTube

I mentioned in the prologue that I discovered scambaiting via the YouTube algorithm, and I would be remiss in not sharing some of the channels that brought me up to speed on what's going on in the scamming industry.

These channels are great because not only can you watch and see how the scams work in action, but you get the satisfaction that comes with scammers thinking they're talking to real victims but, ultimately, coming up empty-handed.

During those hours the scambaiters tie up scammers, you know hundreds of potential victims on those scammers' lists are not being targeted because the scammers are tied up with scambaiters instead.

These channels are as informative as they are entertaining. If you enjoy what you watch on these channels, please consider sharing their videos. One 30-minute scambait video can be enough to spread more awareness and prevent someone from falling for the scam featured in the video.

Also note: Below, I only list three YouTube channels. These aren't the only scambaiters making good content. If you search "scambaiting" on YouTube, you'll find many more. But I've found these three to be the most informative for people who are completely new to scambaiting and scams in general.

KITBOGA

Kitboga was the first scambaiter I discovered, and he was the one who got me hooked. He's incredibly entertaining to watch and his channel is equally as educational as it is entertaining.

Kitboga is known for his role-playing. He calls scammers and can play any number of characters who his fans know by name in any given phone call, so each video is always unique yet familiar to his audience. Kitboga also knows that new subscribers find his YouTube channel every day, so he makes a point of explaining different parts of the scams he uncovers in each video.

While it might be repetitive to some, it's helpful for new people to get them up to speed. In his explanations, he breaks down what's going on, what the scammer is trying to accomplish, what tactics the scammers are using and how they work, etc. That's why I suggest people who are new to scams and scambaiting to start here.

His channel is also family-friendly. He doesn't curse and when the scammers get frustrated at him and curse, he filters their language out. If you're sensitive to explicit language, you should be able to watch his videos without issues.

Aside from educating and entertaining viewers by keeping scammers tied up for hours, and sometimes even weeks and months, doing ridiculous things, he also does his part to slow scammers down by not only wasting their time, but also reporting their bank accounts when he's able to get that information. More recently, when scammers ask him to pay money for fake programs, services, or refund overpayment, he finds ways to corner them into accepting a wire transfer instead of gift cards. And when they provide those banking details, he reports them to the financial institutions they belong to for fraud.

Kitboga's YouTube Channel Link:
https://www.youtube.com/c/KitbogaShow

JIM BROWNING

Jim Browning isn't known for role-playing, but that doesn't make his channel any less interesting. He's most widely known for a four-part series he created in which he tracked down a scam operation, hacked into its phone systems and cameras, and got it shut down by local police. The footage from this series was also included in the BBC documentary *Spying on the Scammers*.

Jim Browning is skilled at hacking into scammers' devices, as well as uncovering their identities and exact locations. He lets scammers connect to his computer and, from there, he's able to reverse that connection and gain access to all sorts of things from the scammers. With this information, he's able to intercept scams, contact victims to let them know they're being targeted, and potentially get some of their money back if money was taken from them.

He's able to do all this without scammers knowing who he is or what he's doing and any information he uncovers from hacking into scammers' devices, he forwards to local police.

Unfortunately, though he was able to shut down a big scam operation, Jim Browning has found that most police departments don't appear to do much of anything with the information he sends them.

Jim Browning's YouTube Channel Link:
https://www.youtube.com/c/JimBrowning

TRILOGY MEDIA

Trilogy Media offers a mix of different types of scambaiting content, but they're most known for confronting scammers face-to-face. Their work is interesting and exciting, but it can also be very dangerous. Still, they're committed to fighting scams, no matter the cost.

Trilogy Media has worked with Jim Browning, Scammer Payback, and other notable people in the scambaiting space to track down scam operations and intercept them.

In a few cases, they've even been able to help some scammers get out of the scam industry altogether and do more productive work.

Trilogy Media's YouTube Channel Link:
https://www.youtube.com/c/TrilogyMedia

GOVERNMENT WEBSITES

UNITED STATES OF AMERICA

The US government has a website dedicated to informing people about the scams being conducted in the US and abroad.

Aside from informing people about these scams, the US government also offers phone numbers people can call to learn more by talking to a live representative, as well as options to file complaints and/or report fraud.

And at the very least, even if you haven't been targeted or victimized by a scam, the US Government's website is still a useful source of additional information.

Source:
https://www.usa.gov/common-scams-frauds

AUSTRALIA

Those who live in Australia can refer to the following sites:

- https://www.counterfraud.gov.au/explore-fraud-problem
- https://www.dfat.gov.au/about-us/corporate/fraud-control

- https://www.ag.gov.au/integrity/counter-fraud

While there are limited examples of the types of scams going around on these sites, there are general categorizations for what counts as fraud, as well as several options for contacting the government for those who've been victimized and/or those who would like to report a fraudulent incident.

Canada

If you live in Canada, you can access more information about scams and fraud through: https://www.antifraudcentre-centreantifraude.ca/index-eng.htm

This website includes information about various scams, including descriptions of types of scams, relevant news articles, information about scam-related legislature, contact information if you've been victimized by a scam or would like to report a scam, and a series of metrics and statistics estimating the impact of scams in the country.

United Kingdom

The UK government released its own book detailing scams - how they work and what to watch out for.

Though the examples seem UK-specific in many cases, it can be a useful document for anyone to read, regardless of where you live.

You can access the book here:
https://www.met.police.uk/SysSiteAssets/media/downloads/central/advice/fraud/met/the-little-book-of-big-scams.pdf

In this book, aside from information about the scams, themselves, readers can find contact information for reporting scams.

Chapter 4. 6 Red Flags to Watch Out For

While there are way more scams than this book could possibly cover, this book offers a glimpse into the most common scams floating around right now.

The good news is there are major red flags that many of these scams have in common.

Though you may encounter a scam I did not explore in this book, there are a variety of red flags that, once identified, can tip you off to a scam.

Regardless of the subject matter or type of scam, there are six key tactics scammers often use to get what they want from victims. And while any one of these red flags, in isolation, might not mean much, a combination of any of these tactics in one encounter will make a strong case for determining whether or not you're being targeted by a scam:

Red Flag # 1: Out-of-the-Blue Communication (For Something You're Not Aware of)

The biggest red flag when it comes to identifying a scam is if a message or request comes to you out-of-the-blue, from someone you don't know, regarding a subject you're neither aware of nor anticipating.

Be wary of requests or gifts you're not anticipating.

The best way to avoid getting scammed is to not open emails from people you don't know and not answer phone calls from numbers you don't recognize.

Scammers know that you don't know who they are, so built into the scripts are different tactics that try to gain your confidence. A request only has to sound believable enough for you to act on it. Scammers know this very well.

Trust your instincts. If you don't recognize the communication you received and/or the person who sent it, consider contacting a third party to confirm the correspondence is legitimate.

If a person claims to be calling from your bank or a government agency, hang up and call the bank or government agency's official phone number directly to find out if the call or email was legitimate.

If the communication you received is unfamiliar to you in any way, take nothing for granted.

Red Flag # 2: Payment Request via Gift Cards, Cryptocurrency, or Money Transfer (i.e., MoneyGram or Western Union)

Scamming is illegal in many countries and is punishable by law. The smartest way to avoid punitive action is to leave no trace.

Why do scammers ask for gift cards or Bitcoin?

Because these methods of payment are completely untraceable and impossible to reverse after payment has been accepted.

By the time you realize you've been targeted by a scam, that money is as good as gone.

The scammer will have sent your money to any number of different wallets that you'll have no way of retrieving your money from. It's pretty much impossible to get your money back without full access to the scammer's crypto wallet.

Please note, however, that there are exceptions to every rule.

Some scammers do accept payment via debit card, credit card, or bank wire transfer. These are relatively normal payment methods for a variety of companies and organizations that accept payment. So, in instances where someone is prompting you to pay money in a seemingly normal way, use your best judgment along with the other signs mentioned in this chapter to help you further evaluate your situation.

Red Flag #3: Instruction to Lie When Purchasing Gift Cards In-Store

If there's nothing fraudulent or questionable going on, why do you have to tell the cashier you're buying gift cards "for your personal purpose" or for a friend, or for a family member?

When a scammer instructs you to pay a fee to them via gift cards or wire transfer, methods of payment that require you to interact with someone (i.e., a bank teller or cashier) in order to complete the transaction, the scammer will instruct you to withhold truthful information.

A legitimate operation won't tell you to lie to avoid "taxes" or "additional fees." But this is what scammers will tell you when you press them about why you have to lie.

If you ask a scammer why you have to tell the cashier you're buying the gift card for your personal purpose, they'll tell you one of two things:

1. If you're dealing with a scam involving a fake legal case, the scammer may tell you that informing anyone else about the case, including the cashier, will result in additional charges or it may compromise your case in some way.
2. Otherwise, a scammer will tell you that if you tell the cashier the full details, the cashier will charge you taxes and fees on top of the money you already have to spend for the gift cards. But out of the goodness of the scammer's heart, they want to protect you from having to spend more money than you already have to spend.

But, of course, none of these explanations are true.

The real reason you're instructed to lie about why you're completing the transaction is simple.

Scammers know the cashier will not process your transaction if they find out you're paying a fee to someone who called or emailed you to pay a fee. Cashiers know what a scam request looks and sounds like, and they have the right to deny scam transactions once they discover them.

The reason scammers instruct you to lie to cashiers and bank tellers isn't to protect you from taxes;

114

rather, it's easier for them to scam you if the people who have the power to stop you from being scammed don't know enough to do so.

RED FLAG #4: INSTRUCTION TO LIE TO FRIENDS, FAMILY, AUTHORITIES, OR ANYONE WHO MAY INTERACT WITH YOU WHILE YOU'RE IN THE MIDST OF BEING SCAMMED

Aside from telling you to lie to grocery store or department store cashiers about why you're purchasing gift cards, scammers will also instruct you not to tell anyone else about the case against you, or the purchase you're making, or whatever else is required to complete the scam.

The scammer will provide you with what seems to be a believable reason why you can't tell a loved one or police officer what's going on.

If you tell a family member or friend that a government official called you about a legal case against you and told you that you need to send Bitcoin in order to resolve the matter, the family member will often try to stop you from completing the transaction. Likewise, a police officer would also try to get involved in a way that prevents the scammer from getting the money they so desperately want to steal from you, and potentially gets the scammer in legal trouble in their own country.

Scammers don't want the time they spend on you to go to waste, so they need you to keep things quiet, at least until after they've made off with your money and left no trace.

If you need to secure your account from hackers, and you have joint bank accounts under your name, the person who you share those accounts with would need to know why you're taking out all the money in those accounts to buy Best Buy gift cards.

But scammers will argue otherwise.

Consider this: If the scammer was making a completely legitimate claim and offering a completely legitimate solution, why wouldn't you be able to tell anyone about it? Though scammers will provide you with fake reasons why confidentiality is important, it ultimately comes down to the fact that if you tell someone what's going on, that person might prevent the scammer from getting any money out of you.

Red Flag #5: Frustration When Asked for Additional Information

The more questions you ask, the more a scam starts to fall apart and make no logical sense.

Think about it: someone just contacted you to give you $1 million out of the kindness of their heart.

Interesting.

But in order to get that money, you have to pay a $200 fee.

Well, that's odd, because why can't they just take that $200 from the million dollars they owe you? It's a drop in the bucket compared to the prize amount, right?

And it's even more odd that you have to buy a $200 iTunes gift card to pay the fee.

Why?

What would they want with an iTunes card when you could give them real money via debit card or credit card?

The more questions you ask, the weirder the mechanics of the scam get—to the point where you realize there's no way it could be legitimate.

But if you ask the scammer all the questions that come to your mind, the scammer will get frustrated.

The scammer becomes impatient with you because the more questions you ask, the more aware you'll become. And the more questions you ask, the harder it will be for the scammer to convince you to part with your money.

RED FLAG #6: FREQUENT USE OF SCARE TACTICS

If you're receiving a phone call or other communication from a government entity or legitimate business, the last thing they should be trying to do is scare you into acting quickly.

But a scam operation, or otherwise illegitimate business, will try to scare you into thinking you need to act right now or face serious consequences. If something sounds scary and your questions for additional information are met with deflection, there's a good chance you're being targeted by a scam.

If you fall for that storyline, the next scare tactic the scammer will use on you is to tell you if you inform any third party about your legal trouble, you'll be in even more trouble.

If you tell the cashier you're buying gift cards to pay taxes, the scammer warns that you'll either face additional legal action, or you'll be charged a higher fee. This is all to scare you into acting and not disclosing what's going on.

If you're dealing with a tech support scammer, the scare tactics usually revolve around viruses and/or hackers. Many of us have a fear of hackers and viruses on our computers stealing sensitive information, compromising bank account information, and taking passwords, etc. This is why we don't click on ads or websites that seem sketchy. This is why we're wary of random links we receive from people we don't know. This is why we use antivirus software.

There are many things we do to ensure our computers provide a safe experience for us. Scammers know that if they can convince you your computer is compromised, they'll have an easier time getting money from you in the name of "removing the hackers." And if they're able to convince you with this scare tactic and they send you to the store to buy gift cards, they'll then scare you into not disclosing to the cashier the real reason why you're buying the gift cards.

These are just a few examples, but they illustrate something important: the more time a scammer spends with you, the more time you'll have to figure out and process what's really going on. They don't want you to figure out you're being scammed before they get money from you.

Plus, scamming is a numbers game, and the sooner they get through with you, the sooner they can get through to the next victim. The more potential victims they can start conversations with, the more money they may be able to make. To speed things up and to get you to comply without asking so many questions, scammers use scare tactics very heavily.

The faster you act, the less time you'll have to realize you're being scammed and taken advantage of.

And the faster you act, the less time scammers have to waste on you, which means they'll be able to move on to other victims faster.

CHAPTER 5. HOW TO PROTECT YOURSELF FROM SCAMS

As long as there are unscrupulous people who insist on acquiring money by taking advantage of people and stealing from others, there will always be scams.

And as long as you have a phone number or email address, you will be targeted by a scam call or scam email at some point.

In terms of stopping scams from targeting you, the chances aren't great that you'll find a 100% perfect solution. However, there are many things you can do to limit scammers' access to you.

Here are a few good tips to start with:

REGISTER FOR THE DO NOT CALL LIST (IF AVAILABLE IN YOUR COUNTRY)

While this won't stop all unsolicited calls because people find new and innovative ways to circumvent the rules, this will cut down on some of the telemarketing calls you might currently be receiving. This is because when you register for the Do Not Call list, companies are required to remove you from their marketing list if you haven't specifically opted in to receive anything. However, not all companies follow these rules. Most scammers don't either.

Violating the Do Not Call registry rules is punishable by law. Companies who still call you even after you register tend to find ways of hiding their real phone numbers. Spoofing, for example, allows a scammer to mask their phone number with a different number so you don't actually know where they're calling from. Other scammers buy temporary telephone numbers that they stop using after a short period of time to further protect them from being caught.

In many ways, the Do Not Call registry will not protect you. But it will reduce some of the unsolicited phone calls you receive.

HANG UP AND/OR STOP RESPONDING

The best rule of thumb is to not answer phone calls you don't recognize, and don't reply to emails from senders who you aren't familiar with. But that isn't always easy to do when you're expecting communication about a job, health screening, business opportunity, proposal, contract work, etc. Regardless, to the extent possible, the best course of action is to only pick up calls or respond to emails from friends, family members, and other people who are saved in your list of contacts.

As much as we all would like to believe we'd never fall victim to a scam, scamming is not a billion-dollar industry for no reason. In the perfect storm of vulnerability and uncertainty, anyone can become the victim of a scam. To eliminate the possibility of a scammer reaching you in a time where you may be vulnerable enough to act on something you otherwise wouldn't, it's best to avoid interacting with unexpected communication, especially out-of-the-blue communication that requires money or personal information from you without establishing that you, specifically, are the intended recipient.

But if you do happen to answer the phone or respond to an email, only to realize it may not be legitimate, the second-best course of action would be to hang up and/or stop responding.

It might be tempting to call back the number that called you to confirm the reason they called, but that's not advisable because if you get connected to anyone at all, it would most likely be another scammer. The number that called you could belong to a scam call center, so if you ask for the reason of the call, any scammer on the floor will be happy to talk through their scam script and see if they can steal money from you.

Many scammers spoof phone numbers, so the number that shows up on your caller ID may not actually be the phone number that is calling you. In some cases, scammers spoof actual government and police department phone lines, which can make the call seem legitimate. But just because your caller ID says the US Customs and Border Patrol office is calling you, doesn't make it so.

By hanging up and confirming the legitimacy of the call, you will protect yourself from potentially becoming a scam victim.

Don't Send Any Money

If someone who you do not know requests money from you, especially if you believe the request could potentially be illegitimate, do not send any money until you are able to confirm the legitimacy of the request. Gather as much intel as you can before you send any money because money sent to a scammer can be very difficult to recover once it's sent.

Scammers are skilled at requesting and accepting payment in ways that are hard to trace back to them, and hard to retrieve once the money has entered their hands. Even with payments that can be traced, by the time you finally realize you've been scammed, it can be far too late to even do anything about it.

Another major problem with sending money is once you send some money, the scammer may add you to a list of people they plan to contact for more money later on. If you've sent money once, that scammer believes you'll send money again. In that scammer's eyes, you could represent a recurring sale if you send money from the initial interaction with the scammer.

Even if that scammer doesn't contact you ever again, that scammer may sell your information to another scammer at a premium because you've demonstrated you're willing to part with your money if the script sounds believable enough. Then, you'll be trapped in a cycle of getting spam calls and sending money you shouldn't be sending to people who aren't offering you anything of real value.

No matter what, regardless of whether you've identified that you're being targeted by a scam or not, withhold any form of payment until you are able to verify that the person requesting payment is legitimate. It's not enough for someone to tell you over the phone or via email that they need payment from you. Do your due diligence. Research the numbers and email addresses that contact you online and contact organizations directly to verify where or not the people who claim to be calling on behalf of them are legitimate or not.

Otherwise, you may find yourself sending money without any real possibility of getting it back once you realize you've been scammed.

CONTACT YOUR FINANCIAL INSTITUTION

The sooner into a scam you realize what's going on, the better. You may have been lucky enough to realize that you were in the middle of a scam early enough in the process to not have given this scammer any of your money. However, if, at any point during the scam, you allowed the scammer access to any of your financial details, you're not out of the woods yet.

Some scammers request debit card information at the beginning of the call but promise not to charge the card for payment until you authorize the payment. However, if you were a scammer whose day job involved stealing from others in order to earn a living, if you have full access to debit card details and you knew your scam operation wouldn't get raided or shut down, what would you do with the debit card?

You'd charge it. Charge it until it declines. Charge it to the limit.

Maybe the scammer didn't request debit card details from you, but the scammer did remote connect to your computer and convince you to log into your bank account to confirm whether you received the refund they claimed to have sent. The scammer even assured you that when you logged in, they couldn't see any of your details. When you typed in your username and password, all they could see was indecipherable symbols.

But that's not true. If you allow a scammer remote access to your computer, they can see everything.

They can see the usernames and passwords you type.

They can also check what pages you have login information saved to.

If you bank with multiple financial institutions and you utilize online banking with each, if you save your login information to your computer, the scammer can access those details in a new window without you even noticing.

Regardless of whether you saw the scammer access your bank account details or not, if you allowed the scammer remote access to your computer for any length of time, contact your financial institution immediately to have them check for new accounts or payment transactions under your account. This way, if they did end up taking any money from you, your bank would at least have that activity monitored, and that would make filing a claim to report the fraud and get your money back so much easier.

Scammers use a variety of tricks to distract you once they get access to your computer so they can try to find sensitive information, explicit pictures, bank details, etc. One common way a scammer may distract you once they are on your computer is by asking you to find a piece of paper and a pen, and then write down a case ID, refund ID, or other string of random numbers and letters. All these ID numbers are useless and don't mean anything. But while you're writing the number down, the scammer is poking around on your computer, trying to figure out how to get as much money from your account as possible without you noticing.

To prevent you from seeing what's going on, a scammer may utilize software to cover your screen. Your screen may appear black, or it may look like your computer is updating. Either way, the scammer has put something up on your screen that prevents you from seeing they are adding a Zelle account or other recipient account to your account for easy access to transfer your money elsewhere.

If at any point you let a scammer onto your computer, even if you didn't see them access your banking details, it's still important to contact your bank to let them know someone may have had access to your financial information. Then, aside from monitoring your account, they can recommend additional courses of action to take to secure your account from future fraud attempts.

Don't Click on Any Strange Links

For some people, when they get an email, their first instinct when trying to determine if an email is relevant to them is to click on a link. In theory, this link will then take them to a website containing more information about the organization or person who reached out to them.

But clicking a link in a scam email isn't that harmless. What you don't know is the link could be masking ransomware, malware, a keylogger, or any other software that, once the link is clicked, will download itself onto your computer and wreak havoc. That software can, then, steal login information and passwords, pictures, sensitive information, and other details, as well as negatively impact the speed and/or function of your computer.

So, if you receive an email you don't recognize, the best course of action is to disregard it. If you're curious, hover your mouse over the link or read your email in text mode so that the link is fully exposed. And if the link looks convoluted or fishy, it's best to not click on that link, no matter how curious you are about what it may link to.

If you're not sure how to expose the link in the email, you can try Googling the email address that sent you the email to find the organization or company it might be attached to. If no official information comes out of your search, the email could be illegitimate.

Additionally, you can Google search parts of the text from the body of the email to determine whether or not other people have received the same exact message. Scam scripts and email copy are often created to be utilized en masse. So, the email you receive could be made up of recycled content sent to other people. And some of those people may have posted the email contents online to warn others about the scam.

Consider conducting Google searches on the email sender and email contents before clicking on strange links. Once you determine the message to be illegitimate, don't click on anything within the email.

Report It

The more you know about a scammer and their operation, the more power you have in terms of who you report to and what the consequences could be. Some scambaiters like Jim Browning are able to gain access to scammers' office cameras, phone systems, and computers, making it easy for them to pinpoint exact locations and other identifying information. Armed with all this information, Jim Browning and others who do the same can report these scammers to their local police departments. More often than not, nothing happens to the scammers. They don't get raided. They don't get fined.

But in some cases, the scam operation gets raided and the scammers get arrested. Jim Browning created a four-part video series where he did just this. With all the information he was able to uncover, he was able to get local authorities involved, which resulted in a scam operation getting shut down.

Obviously, gaining access to the exact location of a scam operation, as well as pictures of the passports and other IDs of all scammers involved in the operation, isn't simple to do. But whatever information you do have is enough to do something with.

If you lost money and/or property to a scammer, you should file a police report and report it to your local consumer protection office if you have access to one.

If the scammer is operating outside of your county or region, your local police department may not directly be able to do anything. But it's still worth filing the police report. If you've wired money to a scam bank account, your financial institution may encourage you to file a police report as well.

At the very least, even if you have no additional information other than the phone number or email address that contacted you, you can report that information to the FTC. Regardless of where the scam is operating, you should always report it to the FTC with as much detail as you can provide in terms of phone numbers, email addresses, messages, subject matter, etc. because scam communications are illegal in many countries and are punishable by law.

Aside from reporting to the authorities, you should also share these scam phone numbers and emails with your friends and family. You never know if their phone numbers and email addresses are also on the scammer's distribution list. By giving them a heads up, you could prevent them from falling victim to the same scam you were targeted by.

Check Your Computer for Viruses, Then Change Your Passwords

For various scams, like the refund scam and the tech support scam, it's common for scammers to request access to remote connect to your computer.

Once they do this, they have access to passwords and login information on sites you may have saved your information to. If a scammer remote connects to your computer, regardless of whether you paid them any money in the end or not, you may think that once you disconnect from the session or shut down your computer, they're gone for good. However, the next time you log on to your computer, they might still be logged in too. Once you log into a bank account, the scammer may not only log your information so they can log into that bank account later, but they may also add their account as a recipient account to your bank.

Aside from stealing your money, the scammer could download spyware on your computer to log passwords or other login information so they can use them later. Out of spite for your lack of initial cooperation, the scammer may also download malware onto your computer to destroy it once they have gotten everything they need from you.

Delete any and all programs the scammer downloaded to your computer. If you're not confident that you know how to do this, have someone else who's computer savvy do this for you. Then, run a scan for viruses and malware.

Once you're sure your computer is clean, change all passwords you have saved to your computer. You never know if the scammer accessed your login information or not, and it's better to not have to find out the hard way.

Chapter 6. Easy Ways to Get Scammers to Leave You Alone

The best course of action is to not answer phone calls from numbers you don't recognize. Likewise, it's best to not answer emails from senders you don't know and trust.

But if you must, the second-best thing to do when you've identified the person on the other end of the correspondence as a scammer is to disengage.

If you're on the phone with them, hang up.

If you're engaging via email, stop replying.

However, if you insist on engaging with a scammer, consider using one of these tactics to get the scammer to stop bothering you:

Ask Plenty of Questions

Though scammers are getting better with the information they're sourcing, they really don't know anything more about you than what is publicly available. If you ask a scammer to confirm your address, they will probably be able to do that because your name, address, approximate age, and phone number are most likely sufficiently documented in public databases.

But the scammer won't know much more than that, so don't be afraid to ask more specific questions.

If the scammer claims you didn't pay your taxes in full, ask what line of the tax form you accidentally overlooked.

If a scammer claims you have hackers on your network, ask which network and what devices are compromised.

If a scammer claims your Amazon account has been compromised, ask the scammer to confirm the email address they have on file for your account.

Whatever the scam, there will be plenty of possible questions to ask.

And the more questions you ask, the more frustrated the scammer will become. Scammers want to get in, get your money, and get out quickly. Delaying this process is not looked upon favorably. After a certain point, the scammer will realize you're probably asking questions because you recognize it's a scam, in which case, they'll hang up on you so they can try to make money off of someone else.

TELL THE SCAMMER YOU DON'T HAVE A LAPTOP, SMARTPHONE, OR BANK ACCOUNT

Many scams rely on you having a computer, smartphone, or other device that scammers can remote access to complete part or all of their scams.

A scammer can't access bank information, passwords, or more personal information if you don't have a smart device they can connect to. If you want to continue talking with the scammer and they express a need to connect to your device, let them know you don't have a computer, smartphone, tablet, or anything they would be able to connect to. This will get many scammers to hang up quickly as their scams depend on remote connecting to a smart device.

Some scammers may try to skip over the remote access part of their scams if you don't have a device to connect to, in which case telling the scammer you have no bank account and/or no money to pay whatever fee they request from you will get the scammer to hang up in no time.

If there's nothing to take from you, the scammer isn't interested in continuing the conversation. With no computer to connect to and no money to steal, you're completely worthless to a scammer.

TELL THE SCAMMER YOU'RE CONTACTING THE POLICE

If you want a scammer to hang up quickly, let the scammer know you're calling the police.

This is not a scare tactic, and if you're hoping this will worry the scammer in any way, the bad news is it won't. Scammers work in call centers all over the world, as well as in their homes. And while scamming is illegal in many countries, law enforcement officers struggle to get this issue under control.

If you knew who the scammer was, you might be able to turn in their information to their local authorities. But if you know nothing about them or where they are, there's not much that can be done.

Scammers know calling the police won't have much of an impact in terms of getting them in any real trouble. Some may even call your bluff and encourage you to call the police, even though they don't want you to actually do that.

However, in most cases, when you mention calling the police, scammers tend to hang up very quickly, if for no other reason than they know you're onto them and they don't want to continue wasting time on someone who won't give them any money.

So, while you won't scare a scammer by threatening to involve your local police department, you will make them cut their losses and hang up the phone.

Tell The Scammer You're Contacting Your Lawyer

I tried this one, myself, on a scam call, but at the time, I didn't know it would lead to a quick hang up.

I used to get fake IRS scam calls multiple times per week. And because I enjoy scambaiting when I have the time, I'll stay on the phone with a scammer as long as I can until they find out I'm just messing with them.

One time, a scammer gave me a fake case ID and I said, "Great, thank you! I'll pass this on to my lawyer to make sure he has it on file."

Before I knew it, the scammer hung up the phone. Now, I understand why.

Scammers don't want any third parties involved, as that could result in the scam not working out. And to get so far in a scam but not receive any money can be a tough reality for scammers.

Realizing I was planning to involve a third party, the scammer decided to cut his losses and hang up the phone. Though some scammers may attempt to call your bluff or instruct you not to involve someone else, most will hang up if you tell them you're involving someone who will recognize that they're a scammer.

CALL THEM OUT

If you want a scammer to leave you alone, let the scammer know that you know they are a scammer.

But be aware that this doesn't always work. A common line phone scammers will say to rebut your accusation is, "If I was a scammer, I would've stolen from you already."

That statement is only partially true because while they haven't stolen anything from you yet, the scammer has every intention of doing so if given the opportunity.

If you call out the different red flags in their scam script, the person will be annoyed and either tell you to hang up or hang up themselves.

Some may try to argue with you or reason further with you, but most will quickly cut the loss and try to move on to the next victim once they realize there's no money to be made by staying on the phone with you.

Every second wasted on someone who isn't going to comply is time that could've been spent scamming someone else.

Pretend to Fall for It, Then Reveal at the End

If you have time on your hands and want to waste a scammer's time, feel free to engage with the scammer and pretend you're falling for the scam. But be careful not to give away any real, sensitive information. And do not let the scammer connect to your computer unless you have a virtual computer and you're confident you know how to operate it.

If you follow the YouTube recommendations I provided in Chapter 3, you'll find videos of scambaiters doing exactly this. The reason I point you to those channels is because they're incredibly educational in that they show you how scammers interact with victims and what things they say in pursuit of stealing someone's money.

These videos also provide a way for you to compare and contrast the things you see in the videos with your own experiences, as well as know what to look out for in those scams you may not have encountered yet.

Some scams are more believable than others. But if you're able to see a scam in action in a video where the scambaiter further explains what's going on, what the scammer's intention is, why it works, etc., you'll get a better idea of both the mechanics of certain scams and what to look out for so you don't fall for it.

I'll admit that when I have the time, I'll purposely answer calls that I know are scam calls.

How do I know they're scam calls?

Some years ago, I moved to a different state, but I never changed my phone number. So, when I get calls from area codes representing where I used to live, and the numbers aren't saved in my phone, I can pretty accurately assume they're scam calls.

Since I no longer live, work, or do business in that area, I'm never expecting a legitimate call to originate from there. Plus, I know scammers often use local phone numbers when they call you to make it seem more likely to be a legitimate call; either that, or they'll use a Washington D.C. number to make it look like they're from the IRS or Social Security Administration for US-based scam calls.

When I get calls from a Washington D.C. area code, since I don't live, work, or do business there either, I assume those are scams as well.

Pretending to fall for a scam and wasting a scammer's time is the easiest way to get a rise out of a scammer. Some scambaiters who share their content on YouTube are able to tie up scammers for over 36 hours; 36 hours those scammers could have spent talking to people who would actually have given them money. When they find out they've been duped, the scammer is quick to express their frustration, even going as far as to curse and threaten your life.

You don't have to answer scam calls, but consider that every minute you spend on the phone with a scammer is a minute the scammer isn't spending talking to someone else who might fall for the scam.

Wasting a scammer's time, in the grand scheme of things, doesn't make a huge difference. Tying up a phone scam for 10 minutes on one random day of the week does little to combat the hours and hours' worth of time scammers put in every day to find and victimize new people.

However, in addition to spreading awareness and sharing this information with your loved ones, it can be a fun and easy way to contribute to driving scammers out of their awful profession.

Chapter 7. What to do if You've Already Been Scammed

By the time you read this book, it may already be too late.

Nearly one in three Americans admit to having fallen for a scam in 2021. And even if you live outside the US, you're not in the clear. Scams are gaining in popularity in other countries, too, like the UK, Canada, and Australia.

If you've recently discovered you were the target of a scam and you fell for it, all hope is not lost. There are a few things you can do to recover from the damage the scammer may have caused you.

Understand You're Not Alone

If you've already been scammed, you might feel incredibly gullible, but you shouldn't. Some people find it hard to believe scammers can be convincing based on the scam scripts and awkward phone calls some of us have been exposed to. But there's a lot more that plays into someone falling victim to a scam than intelligence level.

In fact, it doesn't actually have anything to do with intelligence at all.

Anyone, at any time, for any reason can get scammed. First, understand that you're not the only one and you're not stupid.

Scammers prey on vulnerable people in vulnerable circumstances.

For example, if you recently immigrated to the United States, you may be more likely to fall for an immigration scam.

If you own a computer but you're not tech savvy, you may be more likely to fall for a tech support scam.

If someone you love is struggling with Alzheimer's, Dementia, or other conditions that lend themselves to memory loss, they may be more likely to fall for a refund or healthcare scam.

If you have recently lost your job, you may be more likely to fall for an unemployment benefits scam.

If you're experiencing financial instability, you may be more likely to fall for a government grant scam, or any other scam in which you're offered free money.

The possibilities are endless, but the themes are the same.

None of these examples have anything to do with intelligence level or age. It's true that some populations may be more often targeted by certain scams, and older people and immigrants tend to receive more scam phone calls than other groups, but that has more to do with assumptions about the circumstances affecting those groups than anything else.

Where there's vulnerability, there is a greater potential for exploitation.

If you've fallen victim to a scam, don't kick yourself when you're already down. Neither you, nor the Americans who contributed over $30 billion to phone scam operations in 2021 alone, are any less intelligent than those who haven't fallen victim to a scam.

CONTACT YOUR BANK

If you sent a wire transfer to a scammer from your bank account, or you submitted payment through a scammer's website using your debit card or credit card, contact your bank immediately.

They may be able to get your money back by reversing the transfer or canceling the payment if you catch it soon enough. If you wired the money to a bank account and you still have access to information for the account you sent money to, your financial institution may also be able to help you file a fraud report against the scammer's bank account, which can get the account shut down.

That said, shutting down a scammer's bank account only slows things down. This won't stop a scammer from opening up a new account elsewhere and picking their operation right back up where they left off. Regardless, it's still a good idea to share all necessary details with your financial institution so they can help you understand all your options, and potentially get a fraudulent bank account shut down in the process.

CONTACT THE GIFT CARD VENDOR

If you've come to realize that you fell for a scam in which you purchased gift cards for a scammer, call the phone number on the back of the gift card immediately.

On the back of the gift card(s) you purchased, you'll find a customer service phone number. Call that number to see if they can refund your money and deactivate the gift card. It might be tempting to call the store where you purchased the gift card(s) instead. But if you bought a Best Buy gift card at Wal-Mart, and you go back to Wal-Mart for assistance, they may not be able to issue you a refund depending on where you live, whether you still have the receipt, and whether the gift card was already redeemed by the time you made it to the store.

Scammers work fast so there is a chance that, depending on when you realize you've been victimized, the scammer could have already emptied the gift card(s) before you had a chance to call the gift card company for help.

However, it's still worth trying because even if the gift card(s) are empty, the gift card retailer may still be able to offer you some sort of compensation.

FILE A POLICE REPORT

Often, the scammer you are dealing with may be located outside of your home country or, at the very least, outside of your region.

In many instances, filing a police report won't result in any formal investigation, the return of stolen money or property, etc. However, it's still worth filing a police report if you ever do get taken advantage of by a scammer because your financial institution may ask to see a police report, or encourage you to file one, just in case.

And in the event that the scammer you're dealing with is already under investigation, your additional evidence may help law enforcement crack down on the perpetrator more swiftly and severely.

TELL YOUR FRIENDS AND FAMILY

After realizing you've fallen for a scam, your first instinct may be to keep quiet about it. We don't want to tell anyone because it feels shameful.

We assume no one else is falling for scams, that we're the only person "dumb" enough to be duped. But let the $30 billion lost to phone scammers in 2021 be your proof that you're far from the only one who's been taken advantage of.

By now, you know that vulnerability is the key to the success of the scams circulating today. Vulnerability paired with a lack of knowledge about what's happening is a recipe for continued and potentially exacerbated disaster.

We automatically assume the only people who fall for scams are old people suffering from mental decline, and that stereotype is holding us back from admitting when we've been deceived, lest other people think less of us for falling for something only senile people fall for.

We need to drop that narrative and be more open so other people can be on guard. You do not owe it to anyone to protect them against a scam. But know that sharing your experience and why you trusted the person who took advantage of you, as well as what they said and what they asked you to do, helps the people who hear your story know what to watch out for so they can avoid the same scenario you faced.

Without knowing what's going on right now, how will people know what's real and what's fake?

Even if you're not a particularly trusting person, you're still subject to many of the same vulnerabilities that lead people to unknowingly let scammers take advantage of them. And if you've fallen for a scam, in sharing your story, even if you don't share the nitty gritty details like how much you lost or what sensitive information you provided the scammer with, you're helping spread awareness. If people become more aware of these scams, scammers have fewer people to take money from.

To me, that's a major win.

CHAPTER 8. WHAT CAN ORGANIZATIONS DO TO HELP?

Ultimately, much of the onus is on the individual if they fall for a scam and authorize payment to the scammer.

Financial institutions and payment processors have legal language in place stipulating that if you authorize someone to charge your payment method, that constitutes a legitimate transaction. Likewise, if you purchase a gift card and you give that gift card number to someone, you are authorizing that person to access that gift card.

This means that, unfortunately, if you fall victim to a scam and give the scammer money, there's no guarantee you'll be able to get back everything you lost, or anything at all. Your financial institution or the gift card retailer (if you paid the scammer in gift cards) will try to assist you the best they can, but there may be very little they can do since you authorized the payment.

However, though the onus may fall on you for authorizing payment to a scammer, organizations are not entirely blameless either. In fact, there's so much more organizations can do to protect consumers from scams.

As mentioned, scammers often request payment via gift cards purchased at grocery stores or department stores because those are tougher to track than a credit card payment, debit card payment, or wire transfer. And while there are currently minor protections in place for grocery store and department store customers, a lot more can be done by these organizations to keep consumers safe.

Grocery/Department Stores

In many grocery stores, there are posted signs alerting people about gift card fraud. But these signs are not enough.

At best, these signs are a half-hearted attempt at making it look like the store is trying to do something helpful.

At worst, the signs are just decorations.

If someone is on the phone with a scammer, no sign, no matter how big and colorful, will convince that person to hang up the phone.

Why?

Because scammers often stay on the phone with their victims, occasionally requesting verbal confirmation to ensure the victim is still hooked and complicit.

If engrossed in the phone call, the potential victim won't notice the sign. And if the potential victim does notice the sign and read it out loud, the scammer will offer a rebuttal that might be believable enough.

After all, a person can be far more convincing in an argument than a posted sign.

Grocery store cashiers can deny gift card purchases if they sense something is off, but then the scammer will instruct the potential victim to simply exit this store and visit another one.

I have family outside of my home country and I send money to some of them via Western Union. I've been doing this for years, especially around Christmas time, as this is a big holiday for those relatives who I send money to.

Only once in over six years of completing Western Union transactions did a cashier ask me if I actually knew the person who I was sending money to. Additionally, that cashier explained that she was asking because Western Union's money transfer service is very popular with scammers, and I was sending money to someone located in a country that is known for conducting fraud via Western Union transfers.

I was impressed that someone finally had a thoughtful conversation with me about scam activity, as everyone else who helped me with money transfer activities never questioned a thing.

I don't want to paint a picture that no other cashiers are raising concerns when presented with potential fraud activity, but my experience makes me less than optimistic about how many cashiers are speaking up.

And if the cashiers are speaking up and the posted signs aren't doing the job, what's left to do?

Here are some ideas I've come up with:

GIFT CARD PURCHASES SHOULD PROMPT QUESTIONS

Consumers may hate having to jump through extra hoops to get what they want or need, but it may be worth having a canned set of questions and/or statements to be issued in the event of a gift card purchase.

'Are you purchasing this card at the request of someone who you do not personally know in response to a phone call or message?'

'By purchasing this gift card, you acknowledge that you are not buying it for someone who contacted you out of the blue asking for payment for a grant, lottery winnings, tax payment, or circumstances that you were not aware of prior to receiving the communication.'

Questions or statements along these lines may help expose an attempted scam, which should prompt the cashier to deny the transaction. And if all stores implement these prompts, scammers won't be able to simply send a potential victim to another store to get what they want from that person.

Plus, if a potential victim is on the phone with a scammer while they are trying to purchase gift cards, the cashier would see signs that the victim is being coached if the potential victim defers these questions and prompts to someone on the other end of the phone to get answers.

Stores Could Generate Temporary Gift Cards

In the event that a potential victim realizes they are on the phone with a scammer but doesn't want to tip the scammer off for fear of retribution, stores should have temporary or fake gift cards that they can dispatch to customers.

The cards would come with a receipt and have access numbers, but no money would be exchanged, thus the gift cards would be empty.

Though this would make the scammer displeased, it would give a potential victim multiple opportunities to end the call because they can pretend to have to contact the store to figure out what went wrong. Except the potential victim never calls the store and instead stops answering the scammer until they give up and cut their losses.

Gift Cards Should Display A Fraud Contact Number

The number on the back of a gift card usually goes straight to customer service. It would be nice to see a direct-to-fraud-department number on the back of the card.

In addition to helping the potential victim get their money back, the fraud department would, ideally, also share additional information and advice, including, but not limited to:

- Encouraging the victim to file a police report
- Encouraging the victim to call their bank if financial information was exposed
- Encouraging the victim to contact a professional to look at their computer if they granted remote access to the scammer
- Recommending changing passwords

FINANCIAL INSTITUTIONS

Likewise, there's more banks and other financial institutions can do to protect consumers.

I read a horrifying story about a woman who wired $600,000 to a foreign bank account scammers convinced her to send money to (Lazarus, 2022).

She didn't send it all in one transaction. Scammers know large transfers tend to garner more attention from bank tellers, so they instruct their victims to send multiple, smaller transactions over time.

So, that's what this woman did. Thousands of dollars here, thousands of dollars there, until she had sent approximately $600,000 to scammers.

Representatives at Chase bank did nothing to stop this from happening as they "do not question their customers."

In my opinion, this is unacceptable.

It's important to note that this bank account she was sending money to was a foreign bank account she had never sent transfers to prior to getting involved in this scam. While she insisted she knew the scammers when questioned by bank tellers (thanks to coaching from the scammers), the transactions, themselves, raised enough red flags to warrant further action on the part of Chase Bank.

Scammers won't stop until a victim stops sending them money. So as long as this woman was willing to send money, scammers would have continued to chase her for every dollar she had.

Banks should, at least, exercise their right to inform customers of all financial risks they might be exposed to. A scam can be a huge financial risk.

I understand financial institutions make policies to protect themselves from liability, but at some point, the customer's well-being should also matter.

This isn't to say that banks should block any and all transactions that it flags as potentially fraudulent. However, for every wire transfer, bank tellers should be instructed to follow similar prompts as I outlined above for grocery store and department store cashiers to follow:

'Are you wiring this money at the request of someone who you do not personally know in response to a phone call or message?'

'By wiring this money, you acknowledge that you are not sending it to someone who contacted you out of the blue asking for payment for a grant, lottery winnings, tax payment, or circumstances that you were not aware of prior to receiving the communication.'

A customer may express frustration at being questioned for a transaction, especially if they are on the phone with an impatient scammer, but education is the minimum requirement for financial institutions, in my opinion.

I have the expectation that a financial institution that promises other protections like overdraft protection, for example, will also at least attempt to provide some sort of scam protection that doesn't wait to kick in until someone has lost money and wants to get it back. Prevention should be at the forefront, and the biggest way to prevent scams is to spread awareness and education.

While these organizations might not be able to (and should not necessarily be allowed to) force your hand, so to speak, and prevent you from moving forward with potentially fraudulent transactions, I believe they can and should do more to warn and inform their customers.

Chapter 9. Epilogue

Over the course of this book, you've learned about more than thirty common scams that are currently floating around.

With the knowledge of how these scams work, you'll be better equipped to recognize and avoid them should you ever encounter them.

In this book, we touched on the following scams:

- **Prince scam**, in which a scammer pretends to be a prince or other highly distinguished and noteworthy figure who wants to give someone millions of dollars to help them complete a task to elicit money and/or bank account information.
- **Romance scam**, in which a scammer pretends to be interested in a romantic connection to elicit money from someone.
- **Philanthropy scam**, in which a scammer pretends to be a high-profile individual who

wishes to entrust a potential victim with money to disperse for philanthropic causes to elicit money and/or bank account information from someone.

- **Blackmail scam**, in which a scammer pretends to have reputation-destroying information about a potential victim and threatens to release that information if a fee (often requested in Bitcoin) is not paid.
- **Free car scam**, in which a scammer pretends to have and offers a free car to someone to elicit money and/or personal information that can be sold to other scammers or used to create false identification.
- **Compromised debit card scam,** in which a scammer pretends to contact a potential victim on behalf of their bank to elicit debit card details.
- **Beneficiary scam**, in which a scammer pretends to be a dying patient or the agent of a dying patient who wishes to disburse money to someone as a final wish to elicit money and/or bank account information from someone.
- **Unemployment benefits scam**, in which a scammer pretends to work on behalf of an agency that will disburse unemployment benefits to elicit money and/or personal information from someone.
- **Cash App/Venmo payment receipt scam,** in which a scammer sends fake purchase

receipts to deceive someone into believing their Cash App or Venmo account was compromised to elicit money from someone.

- **PayPal scams**
    - o **Money received scam**, in which a scammer sends a fake notification to deceive someone into believing they have received money into their PayPal account to elicit money from someone.
    - o **Unauthorized purchase scam**, in which a scammer sends a fake notification to deceive someone into believing their PayPal account has been compromised to elicit money from someone.
- **Amazon unauthorized purchase scam**, in which a scammer pretends someone has hacked into a potential victim's Amazon account and made an unauthorized purchase to elicit money and Amazon account details from someone.
- **Refund scam**, in which a scammer pretends to be calling on behalf of a company that owes someone a refund to elicit money and/or bank account information from them.
- **Money flip scam**, in which a scammer pretends that through partnerships with Western Union, MoneyGram, and other money transfer platforms, they can take an initial investment and provide an instant ROI of 2x or

more on the initial investment to elicit money from someone.

- **"Your Facebook account has been hacked" scam**, in which a scammer sends a fake notification to deceive someone into believing their Facebook account has been compromised to elicit money from someone.
- **Love spell scam**, in which a scammer pretends to be capable of casting a spell on someone to make them fall in love to elicit money from someone.
- **Tech support scam**, in which a scammer pretends to offer anti-virus, anti-hacking, and/or firewall-related technical support for a laptop or other smart device in exchange for a fee.
- **Roku scam**, in which a scammer pretends to offer technical support for Roku devices to elicit money from someone.
- **Pyramid scheme**, a business structure in which money from new members is used to financially sustain members at the top of the organization; a pyramid scheme often requires continual recruitment to generate profit off of new members.
- **IRS/CRA/HMRC scams**
  - o **Illegal activity/stolen social security number scam**, in which a scammer claims a potential victim's social security number was stolen and

used for illegal activity to elicit money and/or bank account information from them.

- o **Tax evasion scam**, in which a scammer pretends to call on behalf of the government, accuses a potential victim of not paying the full balance of their income tax, and threatens legal action if the potential victim does not pay a specified fee.
- **Immigration scam**, in which a scammer tries to deceive someone into thinking their immigration paperwork is incomplete or that a fee is required for further processing to elicit money from someone.
- **DEA/Police Scam**, in which a scammer pretends to work for law enforcement and tries to convince you they have a warrant for your arrest that they will execute if you do not pay a fee.
- **Illegal package/US Customs & Border Patrol scam**, in which a scammer claims an illicit package was shipped using the potential victim's name and other identifying details in order to elicit money and/or bank account details from them.
- **Government grant scam**, in which a scammer pretends to be calling on behalf of the government to offer free money to a potential victim.

- **Forex/Investing scams**, in which a scammer pretends to be a successful investment broker and/or portfolio manager to elicit money and/or banking information from someone.
- **Cryptocurrency scams**
  - **Pump and dump scam**, in which a scammer creates a cryptocurrency, artificially inflates the price to entice more people to invest, then sells their stake in the cryptocurrency at a profit, often leaving investors who joined later holding now-worthless cryptocurrency.
  - **Investment scam**, in which a scammer pretends to offer a successful cryptocurrency portfolio management company to entice potential victims to send all their cryptocurrency to the scammer's cryptocurrency wallet(s).
- **Extended car warranty scam**, in which a scammer tries to sell extended car warranty packages that may or may not be accepted at the potential victim's chosen dealership or service center to elicit money from them.
- **Pet-for-sale scam**, in which a scammer generates a fake listing for pets to elicit money from someone.
- **Housing scam**, in which a scammer creates a fake apartment or home listing to elicit money,

personal information, and/or banking information from someone.

- **"Your computer has been hacked"/virus pop-up scam**, in which a scammer deploys a fake pop-up alerting a potential victim that their computer has been targeted by a security issue to elicit money from them.
- **Lottery scam**, in which a scammer pretends to call on behalf of an organization that would like to disburse lottery winnings to someone to elicit money and/or bank account information from that person.
- **"YOU'RE TODAY'S WINNER! CLICK HERE TO CLAIM YOUR PRIZE!" SCAM**, in which a scammer deploys a fake pop-up alerting a potential victim that they've won a prize to elicit money and/or personal information from them.
- **Free gift card scam**, in which a scammer pretends to offer a potential victim a free gift card for only the cost of shipping in exchange for participating in a brief survey to elicit the potential victim's full credit card or debit card information.
- **Kidnap scam**, in which a scammer pretends to have captured the loved one of a potential victim in order to elicit money as ransom.
- **Text message scams,** various scams delivered via SMS message, designed to get someone to act on a fake offer and/or click on a

suspicious and potentially malicious website link.

- **UPS/FedEx package delivery notification scam,** in which a scammer sends a fake attempted delivery notice to get someone to click on a suspicious and potentially malicious website link.
- **Miracle cures/health-related scam,** in which a scammer pretends to have access to a cure or effective remedy for a specific disease or ailment to elicit money from someone who suffers from that affliction in question.
- **Power Company/Electric Bill Scam**, in which a scammer pretends to be from your electric company and tries to convince you to pay a fee to prevent your electric service from being cut off.

Though I have described these particular scams in detail, keep in mind that the scam scripts different scam organizations use can vary slightly in wording and/or mechanics, and this list is not exhaustive.

Though these scams each sound different on paper, scam tactics often exhibit the same or very similar red flags, which include:

- Sending communication out-of-the-blue for something a potential victim isn't even aware of

- Requesting payment in gift cards or cryptocurrency, as these are harder to track, stop, or dispute
- Instructing someone to lie when purchasing gift cards in-store
- Instructing someone to lie or not disclose what's going on to friends, family, authorities, or anyone who may interact with that person while that person is in the midst of being scammed
- Expressing frustration when asked for additional details as to why they're contacting someone
- Utilizing scare tactics to elicit quick and hasty responses from someone.

While these are not the only red flags scam tactics exhibit, you will find that these tend to be the most common ones utilized and the easiest to spot now that you know what you're looking for. If you do spot any of these, you can guarantee you're dealing with a scammer.

If you're amid a scam, and you caught it before it escalated to payment or the release of highly sensitive information, the best things to do include:

- Hang up and stop responding to the scammer
- Don't send any money to the scammer
- Contact your bank so they can monitor your account activity if your financial information

was, in any way, even potentially compromised or visible to the scammer

- Don't click on any unfamiliar links or websites,
- Report the scam you encountered to authorities
- Tell your friends so they're aware
- Scan your computer for viruses and delete any unfamiliar programs, or have your computer checked by a professional, then change your passwords and login information if you allowed someone to remote-connect to your computer at any point during the scam

If you've already been victimized by a scam, all hope is not lost. As early as possible after you discover you've been scammed, consider doing the following:

- Understand you're not alone
- Contact your bank to see if they can cancel or refund any fraudulent charges
- Call the number on the back of the gift card you purchased to see if they can refund your money before the scammer drains the funds if you purchased gift cards for a scammer
- File a police report
- Tell you friends and family so they know not to fall for it should they encounter the same scam

There are many more scams that exist, so this book provides by no means an exhaustive list of what you may encounter.

However, many scam call scripts, emails, direct messages, and text messages utilize similar tactics and tricks, which means the red flags, warning signs, tips, and tricks you've learned will help you avoid other scams I may not have covered in this book, as they will most likely follow the same structures I have outlined here.

Thank You!

Whether you borrowed this book from your local library, received it as a gift from a friend, or purchased it online—I just want to say thank you so much for reading my work.

I've mentioned throughout this book that there are many more scams than I could ever hope to cover here, but the signs to look out for when identifying a scam and the best practices to avoid being taken advantage of apply to virtually any scam out there right now.

I have two favors to ask you:

First, if you enjoyed this book or have feedback to share, please consider leaving a review wherever you purchased this book. The more reviews a book has online, the more visible it becomes to other people who might be interested, especially if the reviews are positive. So, these reviews help boost the visibility of this book, which means more people will find it, download it, and use it to learn how to avoid scams they're being targeted by.

Second, if you know anyone who might benefit from the information provided in this book, I would greatly appreciate it if you passed this book along to them. Consider sharing this book with a friend to help them avoid being taken advantage of by a scam.

Plenty of people have taken to answering random phone calls and replying to random emails to get the opportunity to waste a scammer's time, and that's great. But it's not enough.

There aren't enough scambaiters active right now to tie up every phone line being used to steal money from someone who doesn't deserve to lose it. And while many law enforcement divisions are looking into the reports they receive regarding scams, there's only so much they can do as scammers are becoming better at covering their tracks.

So many scams continue to fly under the radar, so the best defense we have against scams and the best method we have to prevent people from being scammed is to spread awareness.

Thank you for reading and thank you for your support!

APPENDIX

This final section contains scam scripts I found online, as well as scam communications I've actually been targeted with.

Website links, email addresses, phone numbers, and other sensitive, identifying information have been omitted for privacy, as well as to discourage anyone who's curious enough from clicking on potentially malicious links, while spelling and grammatical errors have been preserved for authenticity.

These are not the only scam communications in existence, but these do contain common scam script patterns that will help you identify other scam messages you may receive.

Scam Emails

Hello,

We have temporarily locked your Amazon account and are holding all pending orders.

We took this action because the billing information you provided did not match the information recorded at the card issuer.

To resolve this issue, please verify now with the billing name, address and phone number stored on your credit card. If you recently moved, you may need to update this information with the card issuer.

If you do not complete the verification process within 3 days, all pending orders will be canceled and your account permanently locked.

We apologize for any inconvenience this may have caused. Thank you for your attention.

Sincerely,

Amazon.com

Source: Received by Author

Hi **[email address omitted]**,

Your PayPal account has been temporarily restricted.

You were recently asked to take an action on your account and it looks like we didn't receive a requested response. We have found suspicious activity on the credit card linked to your PayPal account. You must confirm your identity to confirm that you are the owner of the credit card.

To maintain account security, please provide documents confirming your identity. We've also imposed temporary limits on certain features on your PayPal account.

Log into your PayPal account and perform the required steps.

[website link omitted]

Source: Received by Author

Attention: Sole Beneficiary,

The Executive Council Management of International Monetary Fund officially write you after our Executive Council Meeting today over the Following directives change of account petition on your payment file received today on your behalf and we copied to U.S. Department of the Treasury, in conjunction with Office of the Federal Bureau of Investigation (FBI) of United States Fund Tracking Department , as a result of petitions and counter petitions by foreign, inheritance compensation/beneficiaries fund of US$8.5 Million Dollars (Eight Million Five Hundred Thousand United States Dollars) Only non-payment of your claims.

Be highly informed that there are different accounts submitted for your payment by your local representatives in United States by Prof. (Mrs.) Alice Collingwood Nationality (British) Her residential address is: **[website address omitted]** to US-Bank Organization the payment fund bank. We do not know into which account to effect your payment any more since there is a different account number submitted.

Please, you are hereby required to verify the following immediately:-

1. Did you AUTHORIZE one Prof. (Mrs). Alice Collingwood of Britain whose Identification (PASSPORT) Copy is hereby attached below on this

email to claim and receive the payment on your behalf although she claim to be your sister's in-law?

2. Did you sign any "Deed of Assignment" in her favor? Thereby making her the current beneficiary with the following account details below as she present and pose herself to be your sister's in-law:

3. Account Name: Mrs. Alice Collingwood

4. Account Number: **[account number omitted]**

5. Swift Code: **[code omitted]**

6. Bank Name: (BARCLAYS BANK PLC)

7. Bank Address: **[address omitted]**

8. The Transaction Reference: (Your Sister's In-Law)

You are required as a matter of urgency to confirm the legitimacy of the above claim and kindly give us reason why you decided to affect the above Change of Account. If you are not aware of this claim, please confirm to the US-Bank Group immediately by contacting them via bellow email very urgently for legal action to be carried out.

Contact Name: Mr. Andrew J. Cecere

D / L: **[phone number omitted]**

=======================================
==================

KINDLY DO EMAIL ME AT: **[email address omitted]**

FOR INQUIRIES PLEASE EMAIL THE COORDINATOR AT: **[email address omitted]**

FOR PAYMENT DEPARTMENT EMAIL AT: **[email address omitted]**

=======================================
==================

PLEASE FEEL FREE AND FILL IN THE CLAIM FORM BELOW TO ENABLE THE ASSIGNED PAYING BANK TO SPEED UP THIS TRANSACTIONS NOW DIRECTLY TO YOUR OWN DESIGNATED CONFIRMED AND CORRECT BANK ACCOUNT:

(1) FULL NAME:----------------
(2) DATE OF BIRTH:---------------
(3) MARITAL STATUS:---------------
(4) OCCUPATION:---------------
(5) HOME ADDRESS:---------------
(8) COUNTRY:---------------
(9) NATIONALITY:----------------
(10) CELL (MOBIL) NO:---------------
(11) TEL:NO:---------------

(12) FAX:NO:----------------
(13) PASSPORT / ID COPY:----------------
(14) YOUR ALTERNATIVE EMAIL
ADDRESS:----------------
(15) YOU CAN AS BY ATTACHED YOUR BANK
ACCOUNT DETAILS FOR IMMEDIATE RELEASE
OF YOUR FUNDS TO YOU WITHIN 10 MINUTES.
(16) Bank Name:------------
(17) Account Number#:----------------
(18) Beneficiary Account Name:----------------------
(19) Bank Branch Code:--------------------
(20) Bank Swift Code:--------------------
(21) Bank Address:------------------------
(22) Bank Telephone and Fax no (if
any):-------------------------

Due to the long delay this payment has suffered, be rest assured that immediately these payment irregularities are cleared, you would receive your fund immediately.

Note that we are bound to recognize Prof. (Mrs). Alice Collingwood's claim, if you fail to promptly respond/communicate to this inquiry following the Deed of Assignment she submitted to claim this payment. Make sure you get back to us as soon as possible so that the necessary action will be taking immediately without further further delay.

For and on Behalf of International Monetary Fund (IMF)

Ms. Kristalina Georgieva

Managing Director IMF

Tel: **[phone number omitted]**

CHANGE OF ACCOUNT CONFIRMATION
PARTICULARS ON YOUR PAYMENT FILE:

======================================
==============================

NOTICE!

But meanwhile we have urgently managed to
transferred you some part payments of
US$30,000.00 only from the principle amount in
question, in three payments first installment through
MONEY GRAM Express Transfer below are the
Reference Numbers to pickup the payments from any
Money Gram Outlets Agent Nearby right now: Below
are the first three (3) installment payments endorses
to you for easier pickup at any Money Gram Outlets
Agent. Attention please before you can be able to
pickup this funds from any Money Gram Outlets
Agent we still need to authorize and approve this
payment for you first here in our control system
(Computer) so that it can be available for you to
pickup instantly in less than 10 minutes for your kind

181

information: In this transaction each payment is: US$10,000.00 only.

=====================================
=============================

Send Money through Money Gram(MG)

Reference Number: 78461622

Transaction Status: Successful

Transaction Date/Time: 18/05/2020 1:16 pm CDT

From Account: 3354961409 (Current)

Pickup Amount: $10,000.00 USD

MG REFERENCE: 78461622

Sender's Name: Robertson Degbogbahoun

MG Ref#: 75834025

Estimated Destination FCY Amount: US Dollars $10,000.00

Exchange Rate: 1 EUR = 1.09073 USD

Tax Invoice No: 5113-091-150430-125539

GST @1.00000 USD

Transaction Amount: US$10,000.00

Total Amount Payable: US$10,000.00

Purpose Code: Transaction of 1.00000 USD

Test Question: WHAT COLOR

Answer: WHITE

=======================================
==============================

PLEASE DO VIEW THE ATTACHED FILES:

Due to the long delay this payment has suffered, be rest assured that immediately these payment irregularities are cleared, you would receive your fund immediately.

Note that we are bound to recognize Pro. Mrs. Alice Collingwood's claim, if you fail to promptly respond/communicate to this inquiry following the Deed of Assignment she submitted to claim this payment. Make sure you get back to us as soon as possible so that the necessary action will be taking immediately without further any further delay.

For and on Behalf of,

International Monetary Fund (IMF)

Ms. Kristalina Georgieva

Managing Director IMF

Source: Received by Author

My name is Mark Zuckerberg,A philanthropist the Co-founder and CEO of the social-networking website called Facebook,As well as one of the world's youngest billionaire's and Chairman of the Mark Zuckerberg Charitable Foundation which is also One of the largest private foundations in the world right now.I believe strongly in'giving while living' I have one idea that never changed in my mind — that you should use your wealth to help people and i have decided to secretly give {$1,500,000.00} to randomly selected individuals worldwide. On the receipt of this email, You should count yourself as the lucky winner. Your email address was chosen online while searching at random.Kindly get back to me at your earliest convenience,so I know your email address is valid **[email address omitted]** Email me. Visit the web page to know more about me: https://en.wikipedia.org/wiki/ Mark_Zuckerberg/ or you can Google me (Mark Zuckerberg)

Regards,

MARK ZUCKERBERG

Source: Received by Author

OFFICIAL LETTER FROM FEDERAL BUREAU OF INVESTIGATION FBI

CHRISTOPHER WRAY III EXECUTIVE DIRECTOR FBI FEDERAL BUREAU

OF INVESTIGATION FBI NEW YORK.

FBI SEEKING TO WIRETAP INTERNET

ATTENTION: BENEFICIARY,

Please make sure you contact the email; **[email address omitted]** do not reply back to the email sending you massage,

The federal bureau of investigation (FBI) Through our

intelligence-monitoring network has discovered that the transaction

that the bank contacted you previously was legal.Recently the fund has

been legally approved to be paid via UBA Bank Plc.

So, we, the federal bureau of investigation (FBI) NEW YORK, in

conjunction with the United Nations (UN financial department have

investigated through our monitoring network noting that your

transaction with the UBA Bank Plc.legal. You have the legitimate right

to complete your transaction to claim your fund US$3.5,000,000.00 (three

million five hundred thousand united states dollars)

Because of so much scam going on in Benin Republic We the federal

bureau of investigation decided to contact the FedEx Courier Service

Company in BENIN REPUBLIC.for them to give us their procedures on how to sent this money to you without any further complain or delay. We

just got an information from the UBA Bank of Benin Republic and they

have loaded your US$3.5,000,000.00 in ATM CARD and submit to the FedEx

courier service company for immediate delivery to your doorstep.

You are required to choose one option, which you will be able to pay

and also ask them to give you the information you can send the

delivering fee and also convenient for you, for quick delivery of your

parcel containing your ATM CARD and other two original back up

documents. Service Type, Delivery, Duration Charges,Fees

FedEx Express (24hrs Delivery)
Mailing $80.00
Insurance $15.00
Vat $15.00
TOTAL $100.00

DHL Courier (2 Days)
Mailing $90.00
Insurance $15.00
Vat $15.00
TOTAL $105.00

UPS Express (3Days)
Mailing $100.00
Insurance$10.00
Vat ($10)0.
TOTAL $110.00

You are hereby required to advice us, on your parcel delivery option

by filling in the required form stated above. Please note that the

deadline for claiming your fund is exactly one week after the receipt

of this email. After this period, your fund will be return back to the

ordering costumer. That is the instruction given to us.

So take note. We request that you reconfirm your mailing address to ensure conformity with our record for immediate dispatch of your

parcel to you. Only valid residential, Office address and postal

address are certified OK. We are here to protect you from any problem

till you receive your package.You can as well get in touch with the

FedEx delivery company assigned to deliver this financial package to

your doorstep.

Below is the delivery companies contact information:

Companies Name, Federal Express Courier Service

Directors Name: Mr.Bod D.Otega

Email: **[email address omitted]**

Looking forward to hear from you as soon as you receive this message

Best Regards,

Mr.Christopher Wray III
Federal Bureau of Investigation
J. Edgar Hoover Building
935 Pennsylvania Avenue,

NW Washington, D.C

Source: Received by Author

Hello,

i have a colleague who is well established in real estate
and he has just decided to invest in websites and apps
since we have been old friends he decided i help and
guide him to get into it, We are buying and investing
in other ecom businesses as well as this is the latest
trend and it is going to keep on growing each year
with huge profit potential.

We will be making a generous offer of $3k for the
website so you can ignore all other interested parties
and attend to us.

Am a part time tech consultant/broker (mostly to
friends as my side hustle) I have been lucky doing this
and have netted some good profits for myself and my
friends who have invested in businesses with my
advise, my full name is Holly Coburn and Address:
[address omitted]. What i do is we buy a potential
online business, invest in it and grow it to a certain
level where huge returns is guaranteed and then we

190

decide to resell them for much higher than we bought it or continue with the business. We normally invest in the quality of the product being offered, ads, seo, sometimes influencers etc anything that will support and help make the business grow.

My colleague is a millionaire who is new to this kind of business and he want me to guide and help him out, For the payment he said due to bad past experiences he wont go through flippa and would like to send the funds directly to you via bank transfer from his bank, i tried convincing him but as a veteran business man he seem to believe in his old traditional way of doing business i.e bank transfer or checks but i will personally prefer bank transfer to checks due to the long wait time for the check to deliver and also for it to clear.

He would like to pay you by bank transfer. Most of all the businesses i have worked with and made payment to via bank transfer used QUICK BOOKS PAYMENTS to send us the invoice, all of them approved quick books is the best to use for such transactions and we have used that for years with no issues comparing to stripe, authorize and the rest. With QuickBooks you wont have to give out your bank account numbers for the funds to be credited once the invoice is sent and paid the money will be credited directly into your bank account.

If you don't have quick books then visit their website and sign up for a trial so we can use their services to pay you and complete this transaction, you will just sign up like you would for any merchant to use for your business. Once you are set up we can pay you with bank transfer, we would like to close this sale before the end of next week. Below is a link that will explain further:

quickbooks.intuit.com/blog/whats-new/process-ach-bank-transfers-right-in-quickbooks

Kindly sign up with them and get back to me so we can proceed with payment.

Thanks and Best Regards

NB: He told me about why he don't want to use flippa for the transaction, he said he was bulk buying a product from China using an escrow website where Chinese wholesalers and American buyers trade (Just like aliexpress) after all negotiations was done and just after payment was made the supplier told him the money was paid to a wrong account reason they gave was they got hacked and the scammers provided their bank account details and the money was paid into the scammers bank account and not the supplier, after long exchanges he still didn't get his money back and this has happen to him twice in a similar fashion but different methods and all were transactions that has to do with escrow like flippa that is why he wont like to go through flippa.

Source: Received by Author

From Mrs. Linah Mohohlo

The former Governor of the Bank of Botswana.

Reply-To: [email address omitted]

My Dearest in Christ,

Firstly I would like to introduce myself; my name is Mrs. Linah Mohohlo from Botswana. I am the former governor of the Bank of Botswana you can view the profile on the panel members at ((https://www.rhinoconservationbotswana.com/team-linah-kelebogile-mohohlo/).) and read about me. Please I know this may come to you as a surprise, because you did not know me. I sincerely need your assistance discretely because of my high business associations, which is the reason why I write to you on a personal level and through divine direction. It is my

193

desire to have a genuinely personal relationship with you.

I deposited the sum of USD$10.5M (Ten Million Five Hundred Thousand U.S.Dollars) with Finance/bank presently. These funds emanated as a result of an over-invoiced contract which I executed with the Bank of Botswana. Though I am the person who approved this contract but I honestly never knew at the time that it had been over invoiced. presently this money is still with the bank here in South Africa.

I suffer from cancer and recently my Doctor informed me that due to my poor health condition I would not be able to stay alive past the next three months due to the cancer. None the less what disturbs me mostly is the stroke I suffered. Having known my condition I decided to donate these funds to a church or better still a Christian individual that will utilize this money the way I am going to instruct here in. I want an individual person or church organization that will use the funds for churches, orphanages, research centers and widows propagating the word of God and to ensure that the house of God is maintained.

The Bible made us to understand that blessed is the hand that gives, I took this decision because I have a child that will inherit this money but my son cannot carry out this work alone. I therefore decided to use some of the money to work for God and live some for my son to have a better future. My only son is only just 15 year old now and having to grow up without a father he has a low maturity, hence the reason for me taking this bold decision to ask for your assistance. I am not afraid of death hence I know that I am going to be in the bosom of the Lord. Exodus 14 VS 14 says that the lord will fight my case and I shall hold my peace.

I would like you to understand that me contacting you is a divine direction from God; As soon as I receive your reply I shall give you the contact information of the Finance/bank. Any delay in your reply will give me room in sourcing for a church or Christian individual for this same purpose.

Please assure me that you will act accordingly as I stated here and Please I will like you to Reply-me no : **[email address omitted]** immediately you receive this mail so that I will instruct the Finance/bank to transfer this fund into your account.

Remain blessed in the name of the Lord.

Mrs. Linah Mohohlo and only Son Favor.

God's favor is sufficient for me.

Source: Received by Author

I know [password omitted] is one of your password on day of hack..

Lets get directly to the point.

Not one person has paid me to check about you.

You do not know me and you're probably thinking why you are getting this email?

in fact, i actually placed a malware on the adult vids (adult porn) website and you know what, you visited this site to experience fun (you know what i mean).

When you were viewing videos, your browser started out operating as a RDP having a key logger which provided me with accessibility to your display and web cam.

immediately after that, my malware obtained every one of your contacts from your Messenger, FB, as well as email account.

after that i created a double-screen video. 1st part shows the video you were viewing (you have a nice taste omg), and 2nd part displays the recording of your cam, and its you.

Best solution would be to pay me $2648.

We are going to refer to it as a donation. in this situation, i most certainly will without delay remove your video.

My BTC address: **[Bitcoin wallet address omitted]**

[case SeNSiTiVe, copy & paste it]

You could go on your life like this never happened and you will not ever hear back again from me.

You'll make the payment via Bitcoin (if you do not know this, search 'how to buy bitcoin' in Google).

if you are planning on going to the law, surely, this e-mail can not be traced back to me, because it's hacked too.

I have taken care of my actions. i am not looking to ask you for a lot, i simply want to be paid.

if i do not receive the bitcoin;, i definitely will send out your video recording to all of your contacts including friends and family, co-workers, and so on.

Nevertheless, if i do get paid, i will destroy the recording immediately.

If you need proof, reply with Yeah then i will send out your video recording to your 8 friends.

it's a nonnegotiable offer and thus please don't waste mine time & yours by replying to this message.

Source: Received by Author

Subject Line: hopeoj YOur 2022..TraNsunion..EquIfax aNd..Experian..CrEdit-Scores mb

Message: hopeoj Your 2022 Credit score - OPEN NOW!

Source: Received by Author

Additional email examples can be found here: https://www.scamnet.wa.gov.au/scamnet/Scam_prevention-Email_scam_examples.htm

SCREENSHOTS

INVOICE WREQ-7937

INVOICE

$343.67

Paid in Full

View receipt

User

Bill to
User

Invoice details
Invoice no. : WREQ-7937
Invoice date : 05/09/2022

Services	$343.67
Security that includes device security and antivirus programs to help block hackers, a secure VPN to help keep your online activity private, and a password manager.	

Total	$343.67

View receipt

Thank you for your business. You have been charged for Norton Antivirus with Transaction ID:WREQ-7937
If you have any questions regarding your order,

please contact our customer service department at +1 (888) 791-0682

Robert J. Castillo

Delete   Archive   Move   Forward   More

200

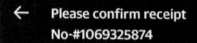

← **Please confirm receipt**
No-#1069325874

Home Depot
to Me
Apr 12, 1:37 PM

Hi, hopeoje CONGRATULATIONS! Details Apply - Expiring Soon: Please confirm receipt No-#1069325874

Congratulation

YOU ARE OUR WINNER!

Delivery fee may apply.

Customer number:

#1069325874

Check what you won

Delete

Archive

Move

Forward

⋮
More

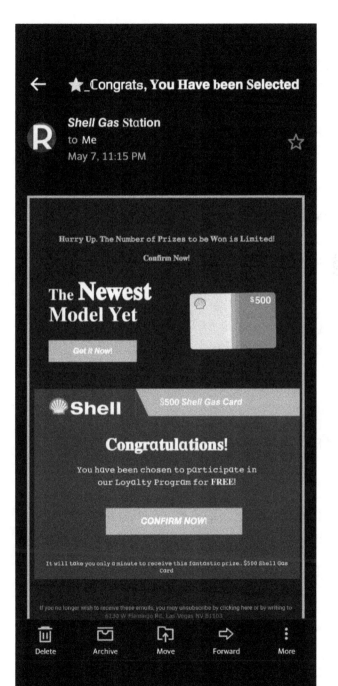

PHONE SCAM SCRIPTS

IRS - Tax Evasion Scam - Full Script:
(https://www.pindrop.com/wp-content/uploads/2014/04/IRS_CompleteCall_Transcript.pdf)

Tech Support Scam - Full Script:
(https://s3.documentcloud.org/documents/2101790/ez-tech-support-script.pdf)

SCAM TEXT MESSAGES

(8kUOVH3mfZEs) Google is re-verifying the phone# of this device. Learn more: **[website link omitted]**

Source: Received by Author

We possibly owe you as much as 628.07. A new finding may have caused us to charge you too much last year. Your savings is ready - **[website link omitted]**

Source: Received by Author

We may owe you up to 512.66. A new decision may have caused us to charge you too much last year. Your savings is ready: **[website link omitted]**

Source: Received by Author

T-Mobile network giving $900 Reward on Covid-19 to all T-Mobile network users. You're free to claim the code and get your reward . Reply YES to claim your Funds . T-Mobile network user Only.

Source: Received by Author

Hope , Millions of fans grief in shock after losing Dr Oz, Hes Gone forever but heres why he will never be forgotten **[website link omitted]**

Source: Received by Author

Beautiful weekend coming up. Wanna go out? Sophie gave me your number. Check out my profile here: **[website link omitted]**.

Dear customer, Bank of America is closing your bank account. Please confirm your PIN at **[website link omitted]** to keep your account activated.

You've won a prize! Go to **[website link omitted]** to claim your $500 Amazon gift card

Source:
https://www.rd.com/list/texts-delete-immediately/

GREAT NEWS: phn# **[phone number omitted]**
earned a free Apple-lPad from your CARRIER. Get it
TODAY. Limited Supplies. **[website link omitted]**
STOP2END

Source:
https://news.trendmicro.com/2022/04/11/t-mobile-t
ext-message-scams/

Hello. We detected fraudulent activity on your Apple
iCloud account. To reset password: **[website link
omitted]**

You received 3 bitcoins ($14, 242 USD) in your
account. Register to accept the transfer: **[website
link omitted]**

Your PayPal account has been suspended due to
suspicious activity. Please contact us immediately at

[phone number omitted] or visit **[website link omitted]**

We are upgrading our database storage facility (NT06117) to a new and better server. To see if you qualify for a FREE upgrade, please provide your username and password.

Source:

https://www.eztexting.com/blog/6-examples-phishin g-text-messages-and-how-fight-back

Scam Voicemail Scripts

Department of the Social Security Administration. The reason of this call is to inform you that your Social Security number has been suspended for suspicion of illegal activity. If you do not contact us immediately, your account will be deactivated. For more information about this case file, press 1 or call immediately our department number XXX-XXX-XXXX

Source:

https://www.ssa.gov/news/materials/pdfs/2019Phon eScamAlertScripts.pdf

----

Good afternoon I will sign and fax an arrest warrant to the department of corrections for your state to revert you to an incarceration facility before the end of the day for violating court orders if you fail to contact the complainant Steve Mason. **[phone number omitted]**

And we're calling in reference to your current credit card accounts. There's no problems currently with your accounts. It is urgent, however, that you contact us concerning your eligibility for lowering your interest rates to as little as 6.9%. Your eligibility expires shortly, so please consider this your final notice. Please press 1 now on your phone to speak with a live operator and lower your interest rates. Or, press 2 to discontinue further notices. Thank you and have a great day.

This message is for (name of potential victim) , my name is Kierra Smith I am contacting you today in regard to your case in the process of being filed in (name of county), case number (xxx).Once the case is filed it does become a matter of public record and

there's an active order for your location.
Unfortunately I was unable to reach you by phone. So at this time I will be contacting your direct supervisor as you are located on the premises of your job. Now you do have one legal right that is to contact the litigation office directly today. That office number that has been provided is 866-205-8355. I wish you both the best of luck. Further action has been scheduled to take place this afternoon.

Source:
https://800notes.com/forum/ta-beb6b13398536f1/scam-call-center-scripts

----

Please listen to this message in its entirety. There is currently a motion being filed to suspend all bank accounts and tax returns bearing your name and social security number. To review immediate rights and details, and avoid all further proceedings, please contact our firm at 1-844-898-XXXX*, or you may press "one" to be transferred to your case manager immediately.

Source:
https://www.fcc.gov/news-events/blog/2019/08/28/

exposing-voicemail-call-back-scams?msclkid=546539
14cf9411ecbc6ee79e85d87612

Kindly revert as soon as possible on our number, that is 804-207-XXXX* - I repeat, 804-207-XXXX* - before we begin with the legal proceedings. Thank you. Have a nice day.

If you wish to speak with our executive, then press "one" now.

Source:
https://www.fcc.gov/news-events/blog/2019/08/28/
exposing-voicemail-call-back-scams?msclkid=546539
14cf9411ecbc6ee79e85d87612

If you are diabetic and using insulin, we can qualify you to get a free diabetic monitor and a complimentary testing kit for coronavirus. To learn more, please press 1, otherwise please press 2.

Source:
https://www.fcc.gov/covid-19-robocall-scams

Hi there, this is Shasta calling in regards to your Volkswagen warranty. The warranty is up for renewal. I'd like to congratulate you on your $1,000 instant rebate and free maintenance and oil change package for being a loyal customer. Call me back at 888-206-XXXX to redeem now. Once again that number was 888-206-XXXX. Thank you so much. Have a great day.

Source:
https://www.fcc.gov/consumers/guides/beware-auto
-warranty-scams

SOCIAL MEDIA SCAM COMMENTS

Retiring from public service made me realize that I had no means of passive income, and in 35 years, I had only moved round in circles financially. I needed to make investments immediately despite retirement and that led me to looking for ways out. I feel very accomplished every time I remember my journey and how I've been able to grow my portfolio to over $500k with the help of my investment adviser Rita Wildrin Mora. Mind-blowing experience really.

Source: YouTube Comment(https://www.youtube.com/watch?v=gktq0Fdobu8)

I'm Paying $4,000 to the first 7people to hit me up now with "HELP OUT"cause it's a blessed month, stay blessed y'all

Source: Instagram Comment (https://www.instagram.com/p/Cdb854kPUqm/)

As a busy person, investing and getting returns was all I ever wanted so I could still retain my job... Although I never believed at first but after my cash out of $19,650 **[Instagram handle omitted]**

Amazing personality with great leadership qualities, I believed in her and success followed. Initially I deposited $1000 and in a couple of days I got $14,500 **[Instagram handle omitted]**

[Instagram handle omitted] My first experience happens to be a total failure but I never gave up cause I knew it was going to work out for me by trying continuously, fortunately I'm smiling today, and it's all because I got involved with **[Instagram handle omitted]** thanks a lot

Source: Instagram Comment (https://www.instagram.com/p/CdbnTRplviB/)

I wish I contacted earlier this year. I'm sharing this to encourage every beginner and Bitcoin lover's to get in touch with her, she is very legit and God fearing person **[Instagram handle omitted]**

Source: Instagram Comment (https://www.instagram.com/p/Cdb-ZhZhoBm/)

RESOURCES

About US - Western Union. Corporate. (2022, May 23).
Retrieved June 11, 2022, from
https://corporate.westernunion.com/

Australian Competition and Consumer Commission. (2021,
August 19). *Investment scams*. Australian
Competition and Consumer Commission. Retrieved
June 11, 2022, from
https://www.scamwatch.gov.au/types-of-scams/invest
ments/investment-scams

Brennan, R. (2022, April 22). *Extended car warranty
scams*. Policygenius. Retrieved June 11, 2022, from
https://www.policygenius.com/auto-insurance/extend
ed-car-warranty-scams-what-you-need-to-know/#:~:t
ext=1%20Extended%20car%20warranty%20scam%2
0calls%20are%20calls,yourself%20from%20predator
y%20warranty%20calls.%20More%20items...%20

Burton, J. J. (2021, November 17). *St. Pete father warns
parents of virtual kidnapping scam after scammers
pretend to kidnap his daughter*. WFTS. Retrieved
June 11, 2022, from
https://www.abcactionnews.com/news/region-pinellas
/st-pete-father-warns-parents-of-virtual-kidnapping-s
cam-after-scammers-pretend-to-kidnap-his-daughter?
msclkid=65d27102ca6e11ecbb27a8553bae5bb1

Chivers, W. by K. (2020, April 10). *Unemployment scams
and covid-19: How to identify scams and help protect
against them*. Official Site. Retrieved June 11, 2022,

from
https://us.norton.com/internetsecurity-online-scams-u
nemployment-scams-and-covid-19.html

Common scams and frauds. USAGov. (n.d.). Retrieved
June 11, 2022, from
https://www.usa.gov/common-scams-frauds

Contributor, F. T. (2020, May 5). *Refund scams: Warning
signs and how to avoid them: Fiscal tiger.* Fiscal
Tiger | Better Information. Better Finances. Better
You. Retrieved June 11, 2022, from
https://www.fiscaltiger.com/what-is-a-refund-scam/

Counter fraud. Attorney-General's Department. (2021,
April 1). Retrieved June 11, 2022, from
https://www.ag.gov.au/integrity/counter-fraud

Explore the fraud problem. Commonwealth Fraud
Prevention Centre. (2020, December 15). Retrieved
June 11, 2022, from
https://www.counterfraud.gov.au/explore-fraud-probl
em

FBI. (2020, March 25). *Romance scams.* FBI. Retrieved
June 11, 2022, from
https://www.fbi.gov/scams-and-safety/common-scam
s-and-crimes/romance-scams

Fraud control. Australian Government Department of
Foreign Affairs and Trade. (n.d.). Retrieved June 11,
2022, from
https://www.dfat.gov.au/about-us/corporate/fraud-con
trol

Gov, U. S. (n.d.). *IRS and Tax Identity Scams: Usagov*. IRS and Tax Identity Scams | USAGov. Retrieved June 11, 2022, from https://www.usa.gov/irs-scams

Gov, U. S. (n.d.). *Pyramid schemes*. Pyramid Schemes | Investor.gov. Retrieved June 11, 2022, from https://www.investor.gov/protect-your-investments/fraud/types-fraud/pyramid-schemes

Government of Canada, R. C. M. P. (2022, June 10). *Canadian Anti-Fraud Centre*. Government of Canada, Royal Canadian Mounted Police. Retrieved June 11, 2022, from https://www.antifraudcentre-centreantifraude.ca/index-eng.htm

Hebert, A., Hernandez, A., Perkins, R., & Puig, A. (2022, May 10). *Scams against immigrants*. Consumer Advice. Retrieved June 11, 2022, from https://consumer.ftc.gov/features/scams-against-immigrants

Hunniford, G. (n.d.). *Personal fraud and how to prevent it | metropolitan police*. UK Metropolitan Police. Retrieved June 11, 2022, from https://www.met.police.uk/SysSiteAssets/media/downloads/central/advice/met/fraud/the-little-book-of-big-scams.pdf

Kaspersky. (2022, June 1). *Common cryptocurrency scams and how to avoid them*. www.kaspersky.com. Retrieved June 11, 2022, from https://www.kaspersky.com/resource-center/definitions/cryptocurrency-scams

Lazarus, D. (2022, January 14). *Column: Chase let an elderly customer wire more than $600,000 to an overseas scammer.* Los Angeles Times. Retrieved June 11, 2022, from https://www.latimes.com/business/story/2022-01-14/column-chase-elder-financial-fraud%23:~:text=A scammer compelled an 81,little to stop the fraud.&text=Seniors lose more than %24600,That%27s shocking and heartbreaking

Leonhardt, M. (2019, April 18). *'Nigerian prince' email scams still rake in over $700,000 a year-here's how to protect yourself.* CNBC. Retrieved June 11, 2022, from https://www.cnbc.com/2019/04/18/nigerian-prince-scams-still-rake-in-over-700000-dollars-a-year.html#:~:text=The%20%E2%80%9CNigerian%20prince%E2%80%9D%20email%20scam%20is%20perhaps%20one,from%20someone%20overseas%20who%20claims%20to%20be%20royalty.

Leonhardt, M. (2021, June 29). *Americans lost $29.8 billion to phone scams alone over the past year.* CNBC. Retrieved June 11, 2022, from https://www.cnbc.com/2021/06/29/americans-lost-billions-of-dollars-to-phone-scams-over-the-past-year.html

Lottery.net. (n.d.). *Lottery scams - common scams information.* Lottery.net. Retrieved June 11, 2022, from https://www.lottery.net/scams

Meskauskas, T. (2022, January 16). *Beneficiary/inheritance email scam.* Beneficiary/Inheritance Email Scam -

Removal and recovery steps (updated). Retrieved June 11, 2022, from https://www.pcrisk.com/removal-guides/19324-benef iciary-inheritance-email-scam

Meskauskas, T. (2022, January 18). *You are our winner today! pop-up scam.* Removal and recovery steps (updated). Retrieved June 11, 2022, from https://www.pcrisk.com/removal-guides/13077-you-a re-our-winner-today-pop-up-scam

Microsoft. (n.d.). *Protect yourself from Tech Support Scams.* Microsoft Support. Retrieved June 11, 2022, from https://support.microsoft.com/en-us/windows/protect-yourself-from-tech-support-scams-2ebf91bd-f94c-2a 8a-e541-f5c800d18435

Mikkelson, D. (2004, December 11). *Government grant scam.* Snopes.com. Retrieved June 11, 2022, from https://www.snopes.com/fact-check/grants-boon/#:~:t ext=Regarding%20the%20government%20grant%20 scam%2C%20keep%20these%20three,extensive%20 documentation%20with%20great%20attention%20to %20detail.%20

NIH. (n.d.). *Beware of virtual kidnapping ransom scam.* National Institutes of Health. Retrieved June 11, 2022, from https://ors.od.nih.gov/News/Pages/Beware-of-Virtual -Kidnapping-Ransom-Scam.aspx

Panda Security. (2022, February 4). *Text message scams: How to recognize, report and restrict them.* Panda

Security Mediacenter. Retrieved June 11, 2022, from
https://www.pandasecurity.com/en/mediacenter/secur
ity/text-message-scams/

TMJ4. (2020, February 26). *Beware of amazon customer support scam.* TMJ4. Retrieved June 11, 2022, from
https://www.tmj4.com/call4action/beware-of-amazon
-customer-support-scam

YouTube. (2015). *Trolling Scammers: I Owe the Dea $50,000 - The Hoax Hotel. YouTube.* Retrieved June 11, 2022, from
https://www.youtube.com/watch?v=4q7lQL357pQ.

YouTube. (2018). *Power Company Phone Scam. YouTube.* Retrieved June 11, 2022, from
https://www.youtube.com/watch?v=fc9EoJN4JZo.

YouTube. (2018). *Watch Out for This Roku Activation Scam During the Holidays. YouTube.* Retrieved June 11, 2022, from
https://www.youtube.com/watch?v=5HMluyQ48qk.

YouTube. (2019). *Behind the Mortgage Closing Scam. YouTube.* Retrieved June 11, 2022, from
https://www.youtube.com/watch?v=SWaZMGSNbKc
.

YouTube. (2019). *Instagram Money Flipping Scammer Revealed. YouTube.* Retrieved June 11, 2022, from
https://www.youtube.com/watch?v=oZNXMoRLPaY.

YouTube. (2020). *I Tried Casting A Love Spell Potion (Scam)*. *YouTube*. Retrieved June 11, 2022, from https://www.youtube.com/watch?v=U0I3uMi-jZQ.

YouTube. (2020). *My Landlord is a Scammer! YouTube*. Retrieved June 11, 2022, from https://www.youtube.com/watch?v=5ihAcwtY-Eg.

YouTube. (2020). *Spying on the Scammers. YouTube*. Retrieved June 11, 2022, from https://www.youtube.com/watch?v=le71yVPh4uk&list=PLBNmQJqxpaMaxqghShRiOnHUjO00ZCsor.

YouTube. (2020). *Watch Out for Puppy Scammers! YouTube*. Retrieved June 11, 2022, from https://www.youtube.com/watch?v=G87SSStG45Q.

YouTube. (2021). *#Dea Safety Tip Dea Phone Scam Psa. YouTube*. Retrieved June 11, 2022, from https://www.youtube.com/watch?v=MtUiH8u7TyI.

YouTube. (2021). *Who Makes Those Scam Popups? YouTube*. Retrieved June 11, 2022, from https://www.youtube.com/watch?v=OkCjz7gdePw.

YouTube. (2022). *Telling a Lambo Scammer I Actually Got the Car. YouTube*. Retrieved June 11, 2022, from https://www.youtube.com/watch?v=z-y5ahvKodo.

YouTube. (n.d.). *Jim Browning. YouTube*. Retrieved June 11, 2022, from https://www.youtube.com/c/JimBrowning.

YouTube. (n.d.). *Kitboga. YouTube.* Retrieved June 11, 2022, from https://www.youtube.com/c/KitbogaShow.

YouTube. (n.d.). *Trilogy Media. YouTube.* Retrieved June 11, 2022, from https://www.youtube.com/c/TrilogyMedia.

www.ingramcontent.com/pod-product-compliance
Lightning Source LLC
Chambersburg PA
CBHW052150070326
40690CB00048B/2228